You Can Get Bitter *or* Better!

You Can Get Bitter *or* Better!

JAMES W. MOORE

Abingdon Press
Nashville

YOU CAN GET BITTER OR BETTER!

Copyright © 1989 by Abingdon Press

This book is printed on acid-free paper.

Library of Congress Cataloging-in-Publication Data

MOORE, JAMES W. (JAMES WENDELL), 1938–
    You can get bitter or better/James W. Moore.
    p. sm.
    ISBN 0-687-46780-2 (alk. hbk) **ISBN 0-687-46781-0** (pbk)
    1. Suffering—Religious aspects—Christianity. 2. Consolation.
    I. Title.
    BV4909.M665   1989   89-32605
    248.8'6—dc20   CIP

Selections from the essay by Wernher von Braun, p. 26, are from *The Third Book of Words to Live By*, ed. William Nichols (New York: Simon & Schuster, 1962). Used by permission.

Excerpts from the article "Death—and How to Deal With It," pp. 39-40, are used by permission of Louisiana Tech University, Ruston, Louisiana.

"Myself," p. 80, is from *The Collected Verse of Edgar A. Guest,* © 1934 by Contemporary Books, Inc., used with permission of Contemporary Books, Inc., Chicago.

"Hug O' War," p. 98, is from *Where the Sidewalk Ends* by Shel Silverstein. Copyright © 1974 by Evil Eye Music, Inc. Reprinted by permission of Harper & Row, Publishers, Inc.

Excerpts from "The Class of 1938 B.C. [before computers]," pp. 113-15, reprinted from the 1983 issue of *Wellesley,* is Copyright © 1988 by Nardi Reeder Campion.

Dag Hammarskjold's prayer, p. 119, is from *Markings,* translated by Leif Sjoberg and W. H. Auden, © 1964 and published by Alfred A. Knopf, Inc. Used by permission.

Scripture quotations are from the Revised Standard Version of the Bible, copyright 1946, 1952, 1971 by the Division of Christian Education of the National Council of Churches of Christ in the USA. Used by permission.

MANUFACTURED BY THE PARTHENON PRESS AT
NASHVILLE, TENNESSEE, UNITED STATES OF AMERICA

*For my family,
and for special friends
who encourage me
to be better*

CONTENTS

You Can Get Bitter *or* Better!

You Can Get Bitter or Better

I t was obvious that the beautiful young woman sitting across the desk from me was deeply troubled. She was nervous, scared, grief-stricken, and heartbroken. And understandably so, because only a few weeks earlier, a tragic farm accident had, in a matter of seconds, made her a widow—a twenty-six-year-old widow with three preschool children. Her bright, energetic young husband had been so strong, so confident, so prosperous, so active, so full of life. But one morning his tractor had brushed against a hot electric wire! One minute, alive, vibrant—full of love and vitality and fun, with great hopes and dreams for his future and for his family—the next minute, gone!

Tears glistened in her eyes as she told me about his fatal accident. Her mascara smudged her cheeks just a bit from the constant dabbing at the corners of her eyes with a dainty handkerchief. The knuckles of her delicate hands were white as she twisted the handkerchief in her lap.

"I don't know how I'm going to make it without him," she said. "But I know one thing: I have a choice to make! I can get bitter or I can get better. And I have come to the church because I want to get better!"

I had never heard it put just that way before, but in a very special sense, she had underscored a universal truth in a crystal-clear way—when trouble comes, when life tumbles in around us, when disappointment breaks our hearts, when sorrow grips our spirits—*we have a choice: We can grow BITTER, or we can get BETTER!*

I once heard Ralph Sockman express it like this: "A grief is a sorrow we carry in our heart. A grievance is a chip we carry on our shoulder." All of us at one time or another must face trouble. It is universal and impartial, and not one of us is immune. There is no wall high enough to shut out trouble. There is no life, no matter how much it may be sheltered or protected, that can escape from it. There is no trick, however clever, by which we can evade it. Sometime, somewhere, maybe even when we least expect it, *trouble will rear its head, thrust its way into our lives, and confront and challenge every one of us!*

The psalmist did not say, "I will *meet* no evil." He said, "I will *fear* no evil." So the question is not "Will trouble come to me?" It will! The question is, "How do I respond to the troubled waters?" The choice is mine, and the option is clear: "Will I let this trouble make me bitter? Or will I, with the help of God, use it to make me better?"

The psalmist put it like this: "So teach us to number our days that we may get a heart of wisdom" (90:12 RSV). Isn't that just another way of saying, "Lord, teach us how to use every day to grow better—not bitter, but *better!*"?

Now let's get more specific by applying this significant option to some of life's troublesome experiences.

When disappointment comes,
we can get bitter or better.

Now, disappointment is a fact of living. No doubt about it. The storms of disappointment come to all of us. As someone once said, our lives are diaries in which we mean to write one story and are forced to write another.

Milton became blind; Beethoven lost his hearing; Pasteur became a paralytic; Helen Keller was both deaf and blind; the Apostle Paul wanted to carry the gospel to Spain, but instead was thrown into a prison in Rome. But were they defeated by their disappointments? Were they embittered? Absolutely not! They all bounced back and turned their defeats into victories! With the help of God, we too can do that! Indeed, this is the spirit of the Christian, the spirit of resilience—the spirit that enables us to *convert defeats into victories, see problems as opportunities, turn death into life!*

I was reading recently about a man who had many disappointments and failures. He failed in business in 1831. He was defeated for the state legislature in 1832. He had a second business failure in 1833. He suffered a nervous breakdown in 1836. He ran for Speaker and was defeated in 1838. He was defeated for Elector in 1840. He ran for Congress and lost in 1843 and in 1848. He ran for the Senate in 1855 and again in 1858. He lost both times, and he was defeated when he ran for Vice-President in 1856. He ran for office only once more. And he won—he finally won one! He was elected President of the United States in 1860! His name was Abraham Lincoln! But Lincoln never became bitter; all those disappointments, and he never got bitter—he used his defeats to get *better!*

Have you heard about the man who lived in a house by a river? Under the house, there was a light, airy cellar in which he kept his prize hens. But one night the river flooded his cellar, and the hens were drowned. Early the next morning he was off to his landlord to announce that he was going to move.

"But why?" asked the landlord. "I thought you liked the house."

"I do," said the tenant. "I like the house very much, but the river has flooded the cellar and all my hens are drowned!"

"Oh," said the landlord, "don't move on account of that. Try *ducks!*"

Now, that's a good Christian story because it reminds us that when one door closes on us, God will open another one. So when disappointment comes, be resilient. Bend a little, and then bounce back! Don't get bitter—get better! Let God, through the miracle of his grace, bring you through that valley and shape you into a better person—not a bitter person, but a better person.

When old age comes,
we can get bitter or better.

There is nothing more beautiful than a person who has aged gracefully. There is nothing sadder than someone who has become more and more cynical, more and more resentful, more and more hostile with the passing years.

At a banquet recently, I heard an elderly man say, with a broad grin and a twinkle in his eye, "I know I'm old because there are three things I can't remember: I can't remember names, I can't remember faces, and I can't remember the third thing I can't remember!"

Now, I suspect the truth is that this man will never really grow old. He is aging gracefully and delightfully, but he never will grow old, because he has that attitude and sense of humor.

Dr. Frank Caprio, in his excellent book *Living in Balance,* has some interesting words about this:

> Growing old is a matter of attitude, not of arteries. You must age—sooner or later you grow aged but you need not grow OLD.
> Old age is nothing more or less than an unconditional surrender to the Old Man with the Scythe. You may make this surrender at forty, at fifty, at sixty, seventy—indeed, at ANY age. But you need not make it at all. Instead, if you will, you can journey through life . . . jousting strong-heartedly with the years, marked but not marred by age. . . . We speak pessimistically of the "declining years," and anticipate a doddering dotage almost as a matter of course. [But it doesn't need to be that way.]
> We keep young by keeping our thoughts young. The body will gradually age: the hair turns gray and thin; the arteries harden; the muscles lose their resilience; the skin wrinkles and loses its bloom. But what does it matter if the spirit is young?   (Arundel Press, 1951 [p. 200])

I saw a beautiful example of that recently. I went to visit a friend who was in the hospital for a checkup. She is ninety-one! When I walked into that hospital room, I immediately caught the zest and joy of her life. The room was bright with sunshine and flowers, music was playing in the background. She was sitting up in bed, writing letters to shut-ins. Ninety-one years old—and she was writing letters to shut-ins!

She explained, "A few years ago I was sick for a week—just long enough to make me realize that these shut-ins must be lonely, not able to get out. So I write to them to cheer them up." Then she added, "I told these doctors to just hurry up and get through checking me over. I've got to get out of this hospital so I can help with Vacation Bible School next week!"

When old age comes, the choice is clear—we can get bitter, or we can get better!

When heartache comes,
we can get bitter or better.

When sorrow comes into your life, don't waste it! Use it, learn from it, grow on it.

Let me tell you about some special friends of mine—Bob and Susan. A few years ago Susan lost her first husband to Hodgkins disease after a seven-year battle. They traveled to the medical center here in Houston forty-three times before he died.

Bob had lost his first wife in a tragic accident while on vacation in the Rocky Mountains. In their sorrow, Bob and Susan found and strengthened each other, and as time passed, they fell in love.

Now, happily married, they have an unusual hobby. They read the newspapers, looking for others who have lost their mates. They contact those people and, with the strength born of their personal bout with sorrow, they help them, minister to them, show them that they too can make it through the valley.

Remember the young woman who lost her husband in the farm accident? Susan was with her that day in my office. Susan found her and brought her to the church—to the place where she had found healing for her own broken heart.

When disappointment comes, when old age comes, when heartache comes, the choice is ours, and the option is clear: We can get bitter, or we can get better.

1

When Someone
You Love Dies

John 14:1-7 "Let not your hearts be troubled; believe in God, believe also in me. In my Father's house are many rooms; if it were not so, would I have told you that I go to prepare a place for you? And when I go and prepare a place for you, I will come again and will take you to myself, that where I am you may be also. And you know the way where I am going." Thomas said to him, "Lord, we do not know where you are going; how can we know the way?" Jesus said to him, "I am the way, and the truth, and the life; no one comes to the Father, but by me. If you had known me, you would have known my Father also; henceforth you know him and have seen him."

The great Christians were not afraid of death; they faced it squarely, confidently, courageously.

"If life is Christ," they reasoned, "then death will be more of Christ. It will not be death at all but the entrance into a larger dimension of life with God." All the great Christians have been very sure of this. History records it again and again.

• *Dietrich Bonhoeffer* was executed on Sunday, April 9, 1945. Later his fellow prisoners in the Nazi concentration camp said that he had been leading a worship service. Just as he finished the last prayer, the door flew open, and two men stepped inside. One shouted, "Prisoner Bonhoeffer! Come with us!" They all knew what it meant: Bonhoeffer was to be executed! As Bonhoeffer walked out, it is said that he told his fellow prisoners, "This is the end. But for me, the beginning of life."

- *Ignatius,* Bishop of Antioch in the early Christian church, wrote to the church at Rome shortly before he was executed: "Grant me no more than to be a sacrifice for God while there is an altar at hand. . . . I would rather die and get to Jesus Christ, than reign over the ends of the earth."

- *Polycarp,* the bishop of Smyrna, about the middle of the second century, was tied to the stake to be burned because he would not curse Christ and bow down to Caesar. Polycarp said, "Eighty-six years I have served him, and he never did me any wrong. How can I blaspheme my King? I am a Christian." Then he said a prayer of thanksgiving to God for the privilege of dying for the faith.

- *Susanna Wesley* was the mother of several children, including John and Charles Wesley. On her deathbed she called her children and their families to her side and told them, "As soon as I am released, sing a psalm of praise to God."

- *John Wesley's* last words were words of great faith: "The best of all is God is with us."

- *The Apostle Paul,* as he faced death, spoke to his Philippian friends with a heart overflowing with joy: "Rejoice in the Lord always; again I will say, Rejoice. . . . For to me to live is Christ, and to die is gain" (Phil. 4:4, 1:21 RSV).

- Then, of course, remember *Jesus'* confident words from the cross: "Father, into thy hands I commit my spirit" (Luke 23:46 NEB).

Now, these are just a few examples of the men and women who faced death confidently and with deep faith and trust. Yet, despite these courageous witnesses (and thousands more like them recorded in history), we must be honest and admit that, more often than not, we prefer not to think or talk about death.

We are something like the man who is attacked by wild beasts and takes refuge in a waterless well. But after he gets into the well, he sees at the bottom a fierce dragon ready to devour him. The wild beasts are above and the dragon is below and he is caught in between. So he catches a branch of a bush growing out of a crevice in the wall. Then to his horror, he sees two mice nibbling at the root of the bush. He knows the branch will soon break off and he will fall into the jaws of the dragon. Then looking around, he sees some drops of honey on the leaves of the bush. So he stretches out his tongue and licks the honey—and for the moment, he completely forgets his very precarious situation.

This old Oriental tale suggests that we too are perched precariously over death—our own death and the death of our loved ones—and, like the man in the story, we choose to ignore it. We refuse to face the hard fact of death; we go through life sipping honey—until suddenly someone we love dies. What do we do then? Most people don't know what to do. Most people don't really know how to handle the death of a loved one.

You know, it is terrible not to know! It is an awful thing to be caught in a crisis and not know what to do. I learned this the hard way when I was a junior high student in Memphis. One year we had a big snow and the schools were closed. One of my best friends was a boy named Bobby and Bobby and I decided to take advantage of the deep snowfall and go sledding on a levee near my house.

We had been there about an hour, having a great time, when suddenly we heard a woman scream and call for help. The scream was coming from behind a house just across the street. Bobby and I dropped our sleds immediately and ran to see if we could help.

As we came around the house, we were stopped in our tracks by an unbelievable sight. An older woman was running across the snow-covered backyard away from a blazing trash can. Her clothes and her hair were on fire. I recognized her. Everyone in the communty knew that eighty-year-old woman. We called her Aunt Bessie. She traded at our family's grocery store; I had delivered her groceries many times.

She ran into the house and Bobby and I ran after her. When we found her, she was sitting at the kitchen table, crying. Her clothes had burned away; smoke and flames were coming out of her back.

We stopped and stood there in shocked silence for what couldn't have been more than five or six seconds, but it seemed an eternity. I can remember as if it were yesterday that awful feeling in the pit of my stomach because I didn't know what to do. Finally, in desperation, we grabbed a blanket off a nearby bed and wrapped it around her, smothering the flames.

Moments later the ambulance arrived, but Aunt Bessie died on the way to the hospital.

Bobby and I were unable to eat or sleep for a few days after that. Of course, we got over it in time, but I never have gotten over that terrible feeling of not knowing what to do, that awful emptiness that comes when you are in a crisis and know that you must rise to the occasion and you don't know how; you don't know how to handle it. It is terrible not "to know."

Yet, it is a fact that many people do not know what to do when someone they love dies. It may well be that we in the church have been neglectful at this point. We have been concerned with helping people sip the honey, celebrate life, find the abundant life Jesus came to bring, and live joyously. And that is as it should be. But we also need to know how to face the crisis of death.

An insurance commerical which ran on television a few years ago showed a youth who had dropped out of college. He told what his father had said to him: "Now, son, you do the studying and I will provide the funds."

The boy said, "It all looked so neat!" Then he added, "But I didn't know Dad was going to die."

We don't like to think of death, but we need to know how to handle it when someone we love dies. With all this in mind, I would like to make some practical suggestions about what we as Christians can do when death comes to a loved one.

*Expect sorrow, but watch out
for those guilt feelings.*

Expect to feel hurt. Expect heartache and loneliness and confusion. Expect to wonder why. We cannot take death as apathetically as a pillow takes a punch.

We know that people die; we know death comes to all. We know that. But it's not quite the same when someone we love dies. When death touches them, it touches us, too. And there doesn't seem to be anything "natural" or "right" about it. They are gone, taken from us. And in their place, there is emptiness. We feel about them the way Wordsworth felt when he wrote about his friend "Lucy: She Dwelt Among the Untrodden Ways":

> But she is in her grave, and, oh,
> The difference to me!

So when someone you love dies, expect sorrow, but don't blame yourself. In fact, you don't need to blame anybody. Sometimes we think that the way to handle a hard situation is to find a scapegoat, someone to blame it on. Guilt feelings make us look for scapegoats. When someone we love dies, we may look for someone to blame. Some may blame it on God, or on someone else, or we may blame ourselves.

On a Sunday afternoon in 1951, my father suddenly became quite ill with a ruptured appendix and was rushed to the hospital. I was thirteen at the time. My brother and sister and I stayed home with our grandmother and waited anxiously for some word.

About an hour or so after they left, the chaplain from Methodist Hospital, who formerly had been our pastor, came to the door and told us there had been an accident—a car wreck—and both our parents were injured and had been admitted to the hospital.

We went to the hospital, but we couldn't find out much—just that our mother was in the emergency room and our father was in surgery. At about ten o'clock that night, the chaplain took us home. He suggested we get a good night's rest, and we went on to bed.

The next morning I woke up early and went out to get the morning paper. And I read in the paper the news that my father had died during the night!

Now, as I think back and relive the experience of sitting there in our living room with the *Commercial Appeal* spread across my lap, I can remember the mixture of feelings that flooded in upon me. I had lost someone I loved. I felt hurt, numb, scared, confused— and I felt guilty!

Strangely, one of the first things I remembered was that only a few months earlier, I had thrown a baseball wildly at a family picnic; it hit my father's hand and broke his thumb. I felt ashamed.

Later, a wise and perceptive pastor helped me to work through those guilt feelings, to realize that the last thing my father, or God, would want me to do was to worry about that. He also helped me to see that you don't need a scapegoat; you don't need to blame somebody when someone you love dies.

Jesus spoke to this once. When the Tower of Siloam fell, killing eighteen people, Jesus was asked (Luke 13:4-5) whose fault it was. Who was to blame? And Jesus said that it was nobody's fault. Those people just happened to be standing in the wrong place when the tower fell.

So when someone you love dies, expect sorrow,

expect hurt and heartache—but beware of those guilt feelings!

Pass on your loved one's best qualities.

It is so important to remember that sorrow and love go hand in hand, that mourning is the by-product of loving. If we love, we will surely know grief.

Look at the Lazarus story. Here is an instance when Jesus was in mourning. He wept when he heard of the death of Lazarus. When the people saw him crying, they said: "See how he loved him." Jesus' mourning was the by-product of love. Jesus was the man of sorrows because he loved deeply.

Then think of someone who will never mourn—a man who lives all alone. He doesn't know where his parents are, and he doesn't care. He has never married. He has no friends and wants none. He visits no one and no one visits him. He cares for no one and wants no one to care for him. Such a man may know self-pity and loneliness, but he never will know real Christian grief, for Christian mourning is the by-product of loving. And it is still true that it is better to have loved and lost than never to have loved at all.

When you lose someone you love, the best way to express your love for that person is to pass on his or her influence. Take up your loved one's best qualities and live them, keep them alive. When my father died, many people spoke of his kindness. Young and old, rich and poor, black and white—all said, in their own way, "Your father was kind to me." The best expression of love I could make to my father's memory is to pass that on, keep that spirit of kindness alive. When someone you love dies, remember that mourning is the by-product of love, and pass on your loved one's best qualities.

Use your sorrow—grow on it, witness through it.

Harry Emerson Fosdick expressed this well in *Dear Mr. Brown:*

> What a strange paradox our life is! We dread tragedy . . . and yet there is nothing on earth which we admire more than a character that handles it triumphantly. . . . Trouble and grief can add a new dimension to life. No hardship, no hardihood; no fight, no fortitude; no suffering, no sympathy; no pain, no patience. . . .
> Don't waste sorrow, it is too precious. . . . Don't misunderstand me. I'm not singing a hymn of praise to trouble. We all alike dread it, but it is inevitably here to be dealt with one way or another. . . . Some people end in defeat and collapse. . . . Others—thank God!—can say with Paul, "We triumph even in our troubles."
> (Harper & Brothers, 1961 [pp. 181-83])

A young missionary couple went to a remote mission station to teach a primitive people about the good news of our faith, but after they had been there some months, the husband was stricken with a terminal illness.

His young wife was heartbroken, but he said to her, "We came out here to show these people our faith, and now we have a chance, a unique opportunity, to really show them how Christians face things and use them for the cause of Christ."

So when someone you love dies, remember the meaning of life. Remember that life is too short for bitterness and wrong priorities; use your sorrow, grow better with it, and witness for the faith through it.

Remember that God is on both sides of the grave.

We belong to God, and nothing can separate us from him—not even death. For you see, death is not really death at all; it is the entrance into a new and larger dimension of life with God. Now, I could quote Jesus or Paul here, but I would rather let a great scientist, Wernher von Braun, tell you why he believes in immortality:

> In our modern world many people seem to feel that science has somehow made such "religious ideas" untimely or old-fashioned.
> But I think science has a real surprise for the skeptics. Science, for instance, tells us that nothing in nature, not even the tiniest particle, can disappear without a trace.
> Think about that for a moment. Once you do, your thoughts about life will never be the same.
> Science has found that nothing can disappear without a trace. Nature does not know extinction. All it knows is transformation!
> Now, if God applies this fundamental principle to the most minute and insignificant parts of His universe, doesn't it make sense to assume that he applies it also to the masterpiece of His creation—the human soul? I think it does. And everything science has taught me—and continues to teach me—strengthens my belief in the continuity of our spiritual existence after death. Nothing disappears without a trace.

When someone you love dies, remember that. Remember that God is on both sides of the grave, and nothing can separate us from him. God is there, and that's really all we need to know. When someone asks me, "What is heaven like?" I feel like that kindergartner who answered that question with "I don't know. I ain't dead yet." Now that answer is not nearly as childish as it seems. It's a sort of futile exercise in supposition to try to imagine the exact nature of the hereafter. All we need to know is God is there!

John Baillie tells of an old country doctor who made his rounds in a horse-drawn carriage accompanied by his dog. One day, the doctor went to visit one of his patients who was critically ill.

"How am I, doctor?" the man asked.

The doctor replied, "It doesn't look good." Both men were quiet for awhile.

Then the man said, "What's it like to die, doctor?"

As the old doctor sat there trying to think of some words of comfort to offer, he heard his dog coming up the stairs. Because the door was shut, the dog began to whimper and scratch at the door.

The doctor said to the man, "You hear that? That's my dog. He's never been in this house before. He doesn't know what's on this side of the door, but he knows his master is in here, and so he knows everything is all right. Now," the doctor went on, "death is like that. We've never been there, and we don't know what's on the other side. But we know our Master is there. And because of that, we know everything is all right."

He loves us, he cares for us, and he has prepared a place for us. He is there—that's all we need to know. When someone you love dies, remember that God is on both sides of the grave.

Remember that God is with you.

God will not desert you. He will hold you up and see you through. He will give you strength you didn't know you could have. This is the good news of our faith, the key message of the Scriptures, the backbone of theology—that God is with us in every circumstance, that God cares, that God knows our prayers before we even pray them, that God is love and he loves us as a father loves his children.

Shortly before his death, Karl Barth made a lecture tour across the United States.

A student in one of our seminaries said to him, "I know you have written volumes and volumes of theology, but can you sum up your theology in a single sentence?"

Karl Barth answered, "Yes! . . . Jesus loves me! This I know, for the Bible tells me so!" When someone we love dies, we need to remember that.

2

When You Feel Rejected

Luke 15:25-32 Now his elder son was in the field; and as he came and drew near to the house, he heard music and dancing. And he called one of the servants and asked what this meant. And he said to him, "Your brother has come, and your father has killed the fatted calf, because he has received him safe and sound." But he was angry and refused to go in. His father came out and entreated him, but he answered his father, "Lo, these many years I have served you, and I never disobeyed your command; yet you never gave me a kid, that I might make merry with my friends. But when this son of yours came, who has devoured your living with harlots, you killed for him the fatted calf!" And he said to him, "Son, you are always with me, and all that is mine is yours. It was fitting to make merry and be glad, for this your brother was dead, and is alive; he was lost, and is found."

There is no pain in the world quite like it—the awful pain of feeling rejected. It hurts! It crushes the spirit and breaks the heart. Let me tell you about a girl I once knew.

Her name was Jessica. She was a tall, slender, sixteen-year-old who looked as if she might grow up to be a model, or president of the P.T.A., or a corporate executive. She was attractive, outgoing, personable, radiant, and happy. She was an only child, and her parents were devoted to her and proud of her. She was a member of a church I served some years ago, and one

Sunday night she did a youth "speak-out" in our evening worship service. As our family drove home, we talked about how she was growing into a mature young lady, about her bubbly personality and that we were inspired by her thoughtful comments from the pulpit that night. She was so wholesome, so full of life.

But the next morning we were jolted awake by the urgent ringing of the telephone. It was Jessica's mother—alarmed, concerned, frightened—telling us that her daughter had been taken to the hospital during the night.

When I walked into that hospital room, it was stark and gloomy. The draperies were closed, the room was dark, heavy despair was in the air. There lay Jessica— only hours before, happy, radiant, full of life—now weak, pale, listless, almost the picture of death. She was so emotionally drained that she literally did not have the strength to lift her arms. She could barely hold up her head. I talked with her for a moment and we had a brief prayer.

As I left the room her mother came into the hall with me. I was anxious to find out what had happened.

Her mother said, "After we got home from church last night, she had a phone call. Just as she hung up the receiver she fainted, and when we revived her she was physically unable to walk, she was so weak. We called an ambulance and brought her here to the hospital."

"Do you know of anything that might have caused this?" I asked.

The mother blinked as tears flooded her eyes. She looked away as she said, "Well, yes. That telephone call was to notify her that she had been blackballed by the sorority she wanted to join."

Now, here was a young girl who, all her life, had had almost everything she wanted. At that particular moment, what she wanted more than anything was to be accepted into that sorority, and one person, for some unknown reason, had blackballed her. The trauma of that blatant rejection was too much. She couldn't handle it. She was not faking; the doctors were sure of that. She was just so hurt that she was emotionally, physically, and spiritually crushed.

Here we see dramatic evidence of "the awful pain of feeling rejected." I want to leave that young woman in the hospital for just a moment; we will get her out later. But the point is clear—the hurt of feeling rejected can be devastating. In fact, the feeling of rejection (whether justified or not, whether real or imagined) is one of the most devastating, depressing things that can happen to us. I am using the phrase "feeling rejected" purposely. The word *feeling* is an important one here for a couple of reasons.

- *First,* sometimes we *feel* rejected when we really aren't being rejected—we only think we are. I heard about a man who stopped going to football games because every time the team went into a huddle, he thought they were talking about him! Now, he wasn't being rejected, but he thought he was. Let me hurry to say, though, that even when imagined, the pain is just as real!

- *Second,* rejection is indeed something we *feel* dramatically—it hurts! Even the strongest persons don't hold up well for long when they feel rejected. Those painful feelings can pull the rug out from under any of us. We see it graphically in Jesus' parable of the prodigal son. There the elder brother is emotionally crushed because he feels rejected.

The younger brother had run away and squandered his money, but then, ashamed and penitent, he returns home. The father is overjoyed! He is so happy he calls for a great celebration.

But when the elder brother hears of it, he is hurt, jealous, confused, angry. He feels sorry for himself—but more than that and worse—he feels that his father has rejected him!

Of course, we know that the father has not rejected him at all. In fact, the parable is misnamed. Instead of the parable of the prodigal son, it should be called the parable of the gracious father! Because, you see, the theme of the parable is not the revelry of the prodigal, nor is it the bitterness of the elder brother. No, the theme here is the goodness of the father—the faithfulness of God. The message here is that God cares, and he wants all his children to come and be a part of the celebration.

But the elder brother missed it. He mistakenly felt rejected, and it deflated and crushed him and left him spiritually bankrupt. The feeling of rejection can do that. It undoubtedly is part of the reason divorces sometimes are more wrenching and devastating than the actual death of a mate. While death brings feelings of deep loss and aloneness, divorce can create overtones of rejection, of feeling thrown away, being unneeded, discarded.

We are told that this also counts heavily in the trauma of a prison experience—the whole aura of being confined, caged, out of touch, out of sight, cut off, rejected. This also is why old age is so depressing to some people; in our youth-oriented culture, they feel rejected. And sometimes when tragedy comes, people may feel that God has rejected them.

The awful pain of feeling rejected—it can crush us emotionally, physically, and spiritually. But the Christian faith has good news for us when we feel rejected—the good news of healing and wholeness. So when you feel rejected, here are a few simple guidelines to remember.

The feeling is temporary.

Don't accept the somber mood as permanent. Remember that this too will pass. Fortunately, in some respects, our moods are changeable, like the weather. That's one of the first things to do in handling the feeling of rejection—remember that it will pass. Dark clouds do come, but behind them the sun is still shining. In time, the clouds will pass, and you will be out in the clear again.

Talk it out with somebody.

There's an interesting old saying that makes a good point: What the average patient wants is not a doctor, but an audience. From time to time, we all need to ventilate our hurts, talk them out with someone we trust. To talk it out with someone who cares, and to hear back from that sympathetic listener some words of encouragement—what a wonderfully healing process that is!!

The person who rejects you
is the one with a problem.

Some weeks ago, I went into a hospital room to visit a little girl who had undergone surgery a few days before. As I walked in, she took one look at me and covered her eyes as if to say, "I refuse to acknowledge your presence!" She was rejecting me because she thought I was a doctor—and she had had enough of them! Her parents and I had a good laugh over her cold shoulder treatment.

Now, that was cute in a four-year-old, but I thought to myself that it was a parable for life. Sometimes when people are hurting, they express their pain like that—by rejecting others! So if someone rejects you, it probably is a red flag. The person who is doing the rejecting is the one with the problem, and you just walked by at the wrong time.

Cultivate a sense of humor;
don't take yourself too seriously.

I recently ran across some humorous answers given by English schoolchildren during religious examinations:

"Noah's wife was called Joan of the Ark!"
"The natives of Macedonia did not believe, so Paul got stoned!"
"The patron saint of travelers is St. Francis of the Seasick!"

"It is sometimes difficult to hear what is being said in
church because the agnostics are so terrible!"

"The fifth Commandment is to humor your father
and mother!"

"Christians can have only one wife. This is called
monotony!"

"The pope lives in a vacuum!"

"Lot's wife was a pillar of salt by day and a ball of fire
by night!"

It's wonderful to laugh with children at the delightful
things they sometimes say. It's fun to laugh at the
comical antics of clowns or the hilarious wit of
comedians. But the best humor of all is a laugh at
ourselves! It's a real mark of maturity; it eases our
self-pity; it diminishes our pride and saves us from
taking ourselves too seriously. Ethel Barrymore said it
well: "You grow up when you get your first good laugh
at yourself."

When you feel rejected, remember that the feeling is
temporary. Remember to talk it out with somebody.
Remember that the one rejecting you is really the one
with the problem. Remember to laugh. And finally:

Remember that God accepts you.

He is with you. This, of course, is most important of
all; it's the key message of the Gospels. It's the real good
news for those who feel rejected! It's the point of the
parable—the gracious accepting, caring, love of God.
William Barclay put it like this in his *Spiritual
Autobiography:*

So then for me the supreme truth of Christianity is that in
Jesus I see God. When I see Jesus feeding the hungry,

comforting the sorrowing, befriending men and women with whom no one else would have had anything to do, I can say: "This is God." . . .

All through his life Jesus was saying to men, and through him God was saying to men: "I love you like that." When he healed the sick, and touched the untouchable, and loved the unlovely and the unlovable, he is saying: "I love you like that." When he endured the insults and the injuries and the treacheries and the disloyalties of men, he is saying to them: "Nothing you can do to me will ever stop me loving you."

(Eerdman's Publishing Co., 1975 [pp. 49-51])

When you feel rejected, remember that God never rejects you. He accepts you. You are important to him. You are valuable to him.

Earlier, we left Jessica in the hospital. Let me tell you what happened. After talking with her mother, I went downstairs and made one phone call. I called the boy who was president of the youth group and told him of the situation. Ronnie said not to worry; he would handle it.

That afternoon I went back to the hospital, and a minute or so after I walked into Jessicia's room, about twenty of our young people poured in! They had flowers, a radio, candy, cards, balloons—all kinds of gifts—and love in their hearts. They gathered around the bed.

Ronnie stepped forward. A hush fell over the room as he (obviously the spokesperson for the group) prepared to say something.

He cleared his throat and then blurted out some words I'll never forget: "God don't never blackball nobody, and neither do we!" His grammar was terrible, but his theology was great.

It was just what the doctor ordered. Jessica smiled and then began to laugh. Each person in that group then came up and hugged her! That day I witnessed a miracle. Jessica went home that next morning! She had been made well by *love*. She had been healed by *acceptance!*

This is the gospel, isn't it? God loves us and accepts us, and then he sends us out as healers, as ministers of acceptance, as servants of mercy, as instruments of his love.

3

When Your Heart Is Broken

Matthew 5:1-12 Seeing the crowds, he went up on the mountain, and when he sat down his disciples came to him. And he opened his mouth and taught them, saying:

"Blessed are the poor in spirit, for theirs is the kingdom of heaven.

"Blessed are those who mourn, for they shall be comforted.

"Blessed are the meek, for they shall inherit the earth.

"Blessed are those who hunger and thirst for righteousness, for they shall be satisfied.

"Blessed are the merciful, for they shall obtain mercy.

"Blessed are the pure in heart, for they shall see God.

"Blessed are the peacemakers, for they shall be called sons of God.

"Blessed are those who are persecuted for righteousness' sake, for theirs is the kingdom of heaven.

"Blessed are you when men revile you and persecute you and utter all kinds of evil against you falsely on my account. Rejoice and be glad, for your reward is great in heaven, for so men persecuted the prophets who were before you."

A few years ago I went to a Louisiana Tech football game. During the course of the evening, I thumbed through the program and was fascinated by how sophisticated these printed programs had become. What once was not much more than a listing of the team rosters and a few advertisements had now become a full-scale magazine.

Intrigued by this, I skimmed through the program,

making mental notes of its contents. Of course the team rosters were listed. There were pictures of the players, with some biographical and statistical information. There were pictures of the coaches, the cheerleaders, the bands. There were schedules, full-page color ads, a president's page, and some well-written and interesting sports articles. This particular program contained an article on how to play the strong safety position; one on "Doc" Blanchard and Glenn Davis, two of the most celebrated college players of all time; another about "Famous Teams That Earned Their Famous Nicknames"; one about women in sports.

As I continued to peruse that football program, I did a double take when I turned to page thirty-two, for there, smack dab in the middle of this college football program, was an article entitled—of all things— "Death—and How to Deal with It"! It was an article on grief. My first response was, "Good grief!" I wondered what on earth that was doing in a football program! As I read on, it became clear. It was a description of a course being taught at Louisiana Tech University by Daniel G. Eckstein. Dr. Eckstein, assistant professor of behavioral science in the College of Education, was trying to prepare students to better understand and deal with the grieving process. The article, written by Pam Wall Ledford, states:

> Grief, not depression, over the loss of a loved one is both desirable and appropriate. And such an expression of emotion is to be encouraged.
> But American culture teaches to the contrary. . . . Stoic strength during bereavement is considered virtuous, and a sedative is an accepted shield to protect the grieved from reality. . . .

>Eckstein encourages students to recall death experiences of loved ones and of pets. He also discusses what he calls "mini-deaths" or traumas: loss of job, separation and divorce. . . .
>
>But death, he admits, is a paradox. It brings sorrow, but it also . . . can become "a moment of your great growth."
>
>Growing experiences are not always pleasant. . . . The comfort factor lies in "the possibility that in the moment of this crisis, families are brought closer together. People get close to the reality of their own death."
>
>These experiences tend to reaffirm commitments . . . to life, life plans and spiritual beliefs.

As I sat in that football stadium reading this, my mind darted back to something one of my favorite professors had said several years before. Robert Browning told his ministerial students never to preach a sermon without a word of comfort, because there always will be somebody in the congregation who is grieving. There always will be someone who has a broken heart.

Now, both Dr. Eckstein and Dr. Browning are right. Grief is a fact of living, and we do need help in knowing how to deal with it, how to work through it. Sooner or later, heartache comes to all of us. Sooner or later, one way or another, each of our hearts will be broken. So the questions fly: How do we get over a broken heart? How do we get through the period of grief? What is grief, and what does it do to us? How does the Christian faith help us as we walk through that lonesome valley?

We can see part of our dilemma in a cartoon strip in Peanuts. Schroeder and Charlie Brown are standing on the pitcher's mound. Charlie wonders why they always lose their games.

Schroeder tells him, "Man is born to trouble as the sparks fly upward."

Charlie looks blank. Linus explains that Schroeder was quoting from the book of Job. He adds that the problem of suffering is a very profound one.

Lucy disagrees: "If people have bad luck, it's because they've done something wrong."

Schroeder returns, "That's what Job's friends told him, but I doubt it."

Lucy comes back with, "What about Job's wife? I don't think she gets enough credit." When the other children join them, Schroeder says that suffering is important because a person who never suffers never matures.

Lucy: "Who wants to suffer?"

Pig Pen says, "But pain is a part of life."

Then Linus tells them that people who talk only about Job's patience really don't understand the book of Job.

As they talk on and on, Charlie Brown steps away from them to comment, "I don't have a ball team. I have a theological seminary."

This reflects the way we dabble around at the edge of the grief process. We often accept superficial, unsatisfactory, unproductive answers—and then seem to be stuck with them. Let's go a little deeper. Let's try to understand "grief" a little better. Then we can deal with it more redemptively when the time comes—as it surely will.

What is grief, anyway?

How would you define it? If you had pencil and paper and were asked to write a definition of grief, what would you write?

Last year I walked into a bookstore and saw a minister friend holding a book and rather sadly shaking his head. The book was titled *The Painful Problems Facing Today's Minister.*

"This is one book I don't need to read," he said mournfully. "I could write this book. I know the problems and I feel the pain."

We all know about the broken heart. We all have felt the pain. We know how grief feels, how it hurts—*but what is it?*

Let me try to define grief. As I understand it, grief is the painful experience of loss. It is the pain we feel anytime we lose something special to us. It is the intense feeling of separation from someone, something, or some place we love very much. It is sorrow, disappointment, loneliness, heartache—and it is not limited to death. It can mean loss through divorce or separation. It can mean loss of a home, loss of health. It can come from loss of a job, loss of face, loss of morality, loss of a friend. All these are grievous. They all break our hearts.

Now, let me hurry to add that when Jesus said, "Blessed are those who mourn," he did not mean that we should languish in a pool of self-pity; he did *not* intend for us to fixate on our tears. I know a woman who lost her only son. When the news came, she pulled down all the blinds in her house. Now, twenty years later, they are still down.

A key point of the beatitude on the blessedness of mourning is the understanding that *grief is a journey.* It has a starting point, and it has a destination. It is something we move or walk through. It's a pilgrimage. The psalmist spoke of "going through the valley of the shadow"; Jesus spoke of the strength that comes from "going through" mourning.

So, grief is a journey. And it takes time to make the pilgrimage, because there are certain stages we need to pass through along the way—and we cannot stay too long at any one place. If we can recognize the stages of grief, it makes the journey easier.

What are the stages in the grief process?

First, there is a numbness, a rather intriguing mixture of shock and strength, almost as if God anesthetizes us to get us through those first difficult hours and days.

Next, there is the stage of expressed emotions—feelings of pain deep down within us which need to be ventilated. Here we often fail miserably, denying the reality of death and the reality of grief, implying that we should be as tough as John Wayne or Charles Bronson. But you see, it's all right to cry. That is not weakness. Sometimes I hear people say, "I know it's weak and selfish of me to cry." But if you hit your thumb with a hammer and tears flood your eyes, no one will say you are weak and selfish. No! You've been hurt! It's painful! And so it is with grief. Deep ties have been severed. You have been wounded and deep emotion is welling up. You need to talk it out, cry it out, work it out, worship it out.

Then comes the stage of loneliness. You feel so alone. The relationship is unique. No one feels it quite like you do—and no one can do it for you. You have to walk that valley alone. And yet not alone, for God is with you and he will bring you through, out of the valley to the mountaintop on the other side.

There is also a period of resentment—anger or questioning. Why? Why did this happen? Whose fault was it? Where was God?

Then, of course, there is the guilt stage, and we find ourselves wishing we could have another chance to do some things (or undo some things) we somehow never got around to—or to say some things. Why didn't I visit more often? Why didn't I call more often? Why didn't I write more often? Why didn't I say "I love you" more often?

Finally, there is the last stage, the return to reality. That's the victory—to be able to pick up and go on with life! As William Barclay put it, commenting on the tragic death of his only daughter: "The one saving reaction is simply to go on living, to go on working, and to find in the presence of Jesus Christ the strength and courage to meet life with steady eyes" (*Spiritual Autobiography*, p. 46).

To be able to go on—that is the mark of faith and victory, and it is the finest tribute we can pay to God and to the one whose loss we mourn.

How does the Christian faith help us?

First, claim the healing fellowship of the church. Let the church family's arms of love surround you. Let the prayers, the casseroles, the tender handshakes, the gentle hugs, the letters, be means of strength. Get back into church as soon as you can and let the church be part of God's healing process.

Next, claim the new power that comes only from having gone through the grief pilgrimage. Those who have gone through sorrow have a new empathy, a new compassion, a new power to help others. The truth is that those of us who have walked through the valley of sorrow have a new strength of character because of that experience; this gives us a kinship with all who suffer and a unique ability to help them. So claim the healing fellowship of the church and claim that strength to help others which comes only from a firsthand struggle with sorrow.

And finally, claim the presence of God. This is what Jesus Christ came to show us—that God is with us and for us. He is a loving Father. Remember the story of the young man whose wife had died, leaving him with their small son? Back home from the cemetery, they went to bed early because there was nothing else he could bear to do.

As he lay there in the darkness—grief-stricken, heartbroken, numb with sorrow—the little boy broke the stillness from his little bed with a disturbing question: "Daddy, where is mommy?"

The father got up and brought the little boy to bed with him, but the child was still disturbed and restless and occasionally would ask a probing, painful question. "Why isn't she here?" "When is she coming back?"

Finally he said, "Daddy, if your face is toward me, I think I can go to sleep now." And in a little while he was quiet.

The father lay there in the darkness, and then in childlike faith, lifted up his own needy heart to his Father in heaven: "Oh God, the way is dark, and I confess that right now I do not see my way through. But if your face is toward me, somehow I think I can make it."

The good news of our faith is that God's face is toward us and he is with us.

4

When Everything Nailed Down Is Coming Loose

Psalm 118:19-24 Open to me the gates of righteousness, that I may enter through them and give thanks to the Lord.

This is the gate of the Lord; the righteous shall enter through it.

I thank thee that thou hast answered me and hast become my salvation.

The stone which the builders rejected has become the head of the corner.

This is the Lord's doing; it is marvelous in our eyes.

This is the day which the Lord has made; let us rejoice and be glad in it.

One day as I passed by the maternity ward in the hospital, I saw a sign that fascinated me—it was a symbol of the changing times: "No visitors. Babies are with their parents." I couldn't help thinking, "My, how things have changed! Just a few short years ago, that sign would have read, 'Babies are with their *mothers.*'"

I remember clearly how they treated me when our children were born. The nurses watched me like a hawk, as if they were sure I was about to do some evil and destructive deed. They made me feel like an outsider or an intruder. They made me feel as if I had a highly contagious form of leprosy. And they wouldn't let me anywhere near the baby.

But look how different it is now. The fathers are

included in a beautiful way. They even go into the delivery room. They are a vital part of the whole process now!

The fact is that things are always changing. Some of the changes are easy to handle, but others are hard to take. But, to be alive is to be in the midst of change.

- *Gail Sheehy,* in her book *Passages,* reminds us that life is a "series of critical passages from one stage to another, and then to another and another."

- *Taylor Caldwell,* in *Let Love Come Last,* points out that even the American Constitution, great as it is, would be impossible if there were no way to add an amendment now and then, because the nation that cannot change will die.

- *Paul Tillich,* the noted theologian, wrote that we are living in a time of "the shaking of the foundations"—and too few of us are ready.

- And as the playwright put it, "Sometimes it seems like everything nailed down is coming loose!"

Well, times have changed and things are still changing, and that scares the life out of some people. Changes are so risky, so uncertain, so frightening.

A cartoon by Jules Feiffer, a cartoonist with a serious intent, underscores how frightening some of the changes can be in our personal lives. It shows a man moving from boyhood to maturity, kicking and screaming and resisting every change, every transition, saying, "I'm not ready!" The last panel shows a grown man hiding in a hole, saying, "I'm not coming out until I'm good and ready!"

Well, it is true that some of the personal changes in life are frightening, and sometimes we do feel like running away to hide. But withdrawal doesn't help; running away is not the answer. There is *no escape* from change. This is true personally, and also socially. Our whole society is undergoing constant change.

A recent newspaper article told of a burglar in Washington, D.C., who robbed liquor stores only in the daytime. When he was caught, they asked him why he only robbed during the day, and he replied, "I'm afraid to be out on the streets at night with so much money!"

Well, times *have* changed! And people are afraid of a lot of things these days—not just at night, but in the daylight too. And yet as someone once insisted, "Education consists in being afraid at the right time."

In some ways, this is a proper time to be afraid. We simply cannot take our civilization for granted anymore! Some things *ought to* scare us. Some things *ought to* concern us. Some things *ought to* alarm us.

Now of course, some changes in our society are needed, inevitable, and overdue. Human rights, scientific adventures and advances, equal opportunity— these are essential. But increased crime, nuclear war, environmental pollution, prejudice, ignorance, physical and emotional abuse, blatant violence—these are sinful, destructive, devastating, deadly things we could well do without!

Times have changed significantly. And the question is, "How do we handle the dramatic changes in life?" The Scriptures can help us. As a matter of fact, the Bible is a book of passages; it's a book about transition, about change and how to meet it.

- We see *Abraham*—leaving his secure home to venture into the unknown, in covenant with God.

- We see *Moses*—leading the people of Israel out of Egypt through the wilderness, toward a new life in the Promised Land.

- We see *Jeremiah*—watching his defeated people carried into Babylonian captivity, shouting to them: "You will be exiles in Babylon for a long time. Don't look back! Make the most of where you are. Learn to live in this strange new place!"

- And we see *Jesus*, saying, "Of old it was said . . . but times have changed, and now I say to you . . . ."

Always and everywhere, the biblical message is the same: You must not lie down. You must move on. You must let go of the past or never find the future. You must not be a prisoner to some old world, lest you never find the new world. You must move beyond nostalgia, or die.

This is what the Scriptures say to us. And if you study them closely, there seems to emerge some very helpful and practical formulas for dealing constructively with change. Let's consider them..

Remember the past—and learn from it!

History has so much to teach us. When we look back, we can learn from the experiences of others—their successes and failures, their insights and misconceptions, their confused notions and dependable principles. And if we are wise, we will learn not to repeat their mistakes! As we recall the past and study history, certain lessons emerge that can be helpful to every age. For example, the past teaches us that love is better than hate; that forgiveness is better than vengeance; that kindness is better than cruelty; that honesty is better than deceit; that peace is better than war. But sometimes I wonder: Will we ever learn?

In *Gentlemen . . . Start Your Engines,* James Armstrong comments about how slow we are to learn from the past:

> In 1755 there was the French and Indian War. We were told to hate the French and love the British.
>
> In 1776 there was the American Revolution. We were told to hate the British and love the French.
>
> In 1799 we fought our sea battles with the French and were told to hate the French again.
>
> In 1812 we fought that war. We hated the British and loved the French.
>
> In 1846 there came the Mexican War. We hated the Mexicans and loved one another.
>
> In 1861 there was the Civil War and the North was told to hate the South; and the South was told to hate the North. . . .
>
> In Korea we hated everyone north of an imaginary line and loved everyone south of the same line. And . . . in Vietnam things [were] even more confused.
>
> (Spiritual Life Publishers, 1967)

Now, I don't know how you feel about Armstrong's words, but I do know that we learned in Sunday school a long time ago, from the teachings of Jesus, not to hate anybody! We can't go back in time, but in facing the ever-present changes constantly exploding into our lives, we can assess them and deal with them more creatively if we can remember the past—and *learn from it!*

Relish the present—and ·live in it!

Do you remember the Sensitivity Movement in the 60s and 70s? It had its problems, to be sure, but it did challenge us to be more aware of what is happening around us, to be more sensitive to what's going on, to get in touch with our feelings. We need to work on that, because we do tend to insulate ourselves from the outside world. We are victims of implosion! Explosion means things exploding out; implosion means things exploding in.

So much is happening. So much is exploding in on us at such a rapid, frantic, hectic pace that we tune out. We forget how to feel! We forget how to smell the roses. We forget how to celebrate the present. We forget how to live in the now. We forget how to relish the moment.

This is at least a part of what Jesus meant when he said that unless we become like little children, we will miss the kingdom. Children know how to relish the moment because they know how to feel, how to experience things. We *know about* things. But children *experience* things! Have you ever seen a child experience ice cream or cotton candy? Have you ever seen a child touch a puppy—and squeal with delight when the puppy responds? We are much too sophisticated to become excited about things like that.

Recently I was in a restaurant for breakfast when I saw a small boy experience grits. Now, he didn't just eat the grits; he experienced them—with his hands, with his arms, on his nose, in his ears, in his hair, all over his clothes and on his dad's new tie. He touched, tasted, and felt grits. He *experienced* grits!

Then consider the man who visited the South for the first time. He ordered breakfast.

The waitress said, "Don't you want some grits?"

The man answered, "No."

The waitress persisted. "But grits are wonderful. Why don't you try them? Let me serve you some grits!"

"Oh, all right," said the man, "but bring me just one!"

That's our problem, isn't it? We ask for just one grit! We have become so sophisticated, so set in our ways, so insulated, so turned off and tuned out.

But Jesus calls us to be like little children—to celebrate life, to be aware, to relish the present and live in it! The psalmist said it: "This is the day which the LORD has made; let us rejoice and be glad in it!"

Respond to the future—and lean toward it!

Years ago I played football. I was a back, and the first thing the coaches taught us was how to "run with a forward lean," to run leaning forward, so that even when knocked down, we could gain valuable yardage. That's a good parable for life, isn't it? As Christians, we can live with a forward lean. We can remember the past and learn from it. We can relish the present and live in it. And we can respond to the future and lean toward it.

I have a younger sister named Susie. When Susie was two years old, we had a very perplexing problem. She was just fine during the day, but at night she would cry and complain that her legs hurt. We feared the worst and took her to the doctor. He examined her carefully and could find no problem. She was in perfect health.

But that night, it happened again. She cried at bedtime and complained convincingly that her legs were hurting. Well, finally we figured it out. She was wearing those pajamas with feet in them, and she had outgrown them! Her legs were cramped by her too-short pajamas!

We need room to grow toward the future! And the way to get that room is to keep our minds open to the incredible possibilities of God's future! As the gospel songwriter put it, "We know not what the future holds, but we know who holds the future!"

5

When You Feel Trapped by Your Fears

Mark 10:17-22 And as he was setting out on his journey, a man ran up and knelt before him, and asked him, "Good Teacher, what must I do to inherit eternal life?" And Jesus said to him, "Why do you call me good? No one is good but God alone. You know the commandments: 'Do not kill, Do not commit adultery, Do not steal, Do not bear false witness, Do not defraud, Honor your father and mother.'" And he said to him, "Teacher, all these I have observed from my youth." And Jesus looking upon him loved him, and said to him, "You lack one thing; go, sell what you have, and give to the poor, and you will have treasure in heaven; and come, follow me." At that saying his countenance fell, and he went away sorrowful; for he had great possessions.

In the late 1960s in a small southern town, a middle-aged woman became desperately frightened. She was morbidly afraid that burglars would break into her home. It may have been because of so much TV violence, or news reports on increases in the crime rate, or rumors around town of numerous break-ins—or a combination of these.

Whatever the reason, she became so frightened that her fears mushroomed to the point of paranoia. She pleaded with her husband to bar the windows and doors. In the hope of easing her mind, he finally agreed and had heavy bars attached securely to all the windows and doors.

Still she was frightened, so she talked her husband into adding additional strands of steel over the window bars, making it almost impossible for anyone to gain entry to the house. Virtually sealed off from the outside world, she felt safer, much more secure.

But one afternoon while she was taking a nap, the house caught fire and she awakened to find herself trapped! Her husband, the fire department, the police, the emergency squad, and concerned neighbors all worked frantically to get her out of the burning house, to no avail. They could not remove the heavy bars in time. Tragically, she lost her life—trapped by her own fears, trapped in a prison of her own making!

In a different sense and on a different level, could this be true of us? Is that woman's tragic experience a parable for us? Do we have fears or attitudes or weaknesses that imprison us? Do we have crippling phobias or anxieties that cut us off from life, from other people, from the church, from God? Are we free to live fully, as God intended? Or are we trapped and paralyzed and imprisoned by our fears?

Recently while leading a youth retreat, I asked the young people to anonymously complete this open-ended sentence: "Being a teenager in today's world is like . . . ." Some of their responses were remarkable and revealing:

"Being a teenager in today's world is like soaring through space in a rocketship, knowing the right buttons to push, but somehow being unable to push them."

"Being a teenager in today's world is like standing in the wings of a great stage called life, wanting so much to go out on the stage and be a big hit but feeling paralyzed by stage fright."

"Being a teenager in today's world is like being a bird and wanting to spread my wings and fly but scared to leave the safety of my warm, secure nest."

"Being a teenager in today's world is like wanting to reach out and touch the world, but afraid of reaching out too soon and afraid of being touched back too deeply or too suddenly."

There we see it—the longing of young people to touch the world, to taste life; but afraid—afraid of the risks, the demands, the responsibilities. Does that sound familiar to you? It reminds me of something I've felt. It reminds me of something I've seen in others. And it reminds me of something in the Bible.

In the tenth chapter of Mark's Gospel, we find two contrasting stories, two of Christ's most interesting encounters—the rich young ruler and blind Bartimaeus.

THE RICH YOUNG RULER. Jesus is on his way to Jerusalem, on his way to the cross, when the rich young ruler runs up and kneels before him. Notice this: "He runs up"—a sign of enthusiasm; "He kneels"—a sign of respect and reverence.

Thus we can assume here that this young man is not trying to trap Jesus with a loaded question (as others tried), but that he is really sincere.

He asks, "Good Teacher, what must I do to inherit eternal life?"

Jesus answers, "You know the commandments: 'Do not kill, Do not commit adultery, Do not steal, Do not bear false witness, Do not defraud, Honor your father and mother.'"

The young man answers, "All these I have observed from my youth."

Jesus then looks at him with love. "You lack one thing; go, sell what you have, and give to the poor, and you will have treasure in heaven; and come, follow me."

At this, the rich young ruler turns away and leaves sorrowfully, trapped in a prison of his own making, trapped by his own fears.

BUT REMEMBER BLIND BARTIMAEUS. What a contrast! Jesus is leaving Jericho with his disciples. A great crowd is pressing in upon him amid lots of noise and commotion.

Bartimaeus, a blind beggar, is sitting by the roadside. His cloak is spread before him, so that sympathetic passers-by might toss a few coins on it, enabling him to survive a few more days.

Evidently he had heard of Jesus, because as Jesus comes by, he begins to cry out, "Jesus, Son of David, have mercy on me!"

The crowd tries to shush him. They think Jesus is too busy to be bothered by this poor wretched beggar. But Bartimaeus will not be denied. He cries out more desperately. And suddenly Jesus stops. He has heard the cries. Somehow over the noise of the crowd, he hears Bartimaeus, and he calls him.

Bartimaeus throws his cloak aside. The coins on it fall into the dust. Bartimaeus doesn't care about the money now. All that matters is to reach the Master. The

Scriptures go on to tell us that Jesus restored the man's sight and that Bartimaeus "followed him on the way."

Two men—the rich young ruler and blind Bartimaeus. One misses out, trapped by his fears; the other finds new vision and new life.

"Wait!" you may say. "The rich young ruler had more to lose; blind Bartimaeus had everything to gain!"

Jesus recognized this, too—that it is hard for those who are secure and comfortable to really commit themselves.

He said, "How hard it will be for those who have riches to enter the kingdom." It's not wrong to have riches, as long as our riches do not imprison us and keep us from Christ.

The question is, which of these two possibilities do we identify with? Sometimes we are trapped, imprisoned, paralyzed by our own fears.

We can be trapped by our fear of commitment.

In a graveyard in West Virginia, there is a tombstone with this inscription:

> I've gone ahead as you can see,
> So trust my lead and follow me.

Some wag came along later and wrote beneath it:

> To follow you I am not content,
> Until I know which way you went!

This is a light treatment of a significant point—namely, that because of the credibility gap, we are cautious about making commitments. And that's good, up to a point. We do need to be careful, but sometimes I think we can become so guarded, so frightened, that we are afraid to commit ourselves to anyone or any-thing—and that is tragic.

In the early days of the church, a young Christian was arrested for "preaching Christ." He was shown the headman's axe and told that unless he renounced his loyalty to Christ, he would be beheaded on the spot.

With tenacious commitment, he turned to his adversaries and said, "You can take my head from my shoulders, but you will never take my heart from my King!"

Now that's real commitment! Think what would happen if every member of the church had that kind of commitment! It would change not only the church—it would change the whole world! The rich young ruler turned away sorrowfully because he could not make a commitment. Sometimes, neither can we, and that is sorrowful.

We can be trapped by our fear of embarrassment.

That is one of the great things about Bartimaeus. He did not let fear of embarrassment stop him. That was his moment! He did not let pride imprison him. He cried out unashamedly. Here was his chance, and he would not be denied!

Some months ago a young man showed up at the church. A year or so before, he had gotten into trouble with drugs. There had been a tough confrontation with his father, a heated argument, harsh words were spoken, and in a rage, this young man had run away from home. Last Christmas he went back home, but he didn't go into the house. He stood outside in the snow and looked in the window. He saw his family having

Christmas dinner before the fireplace. He wanted to go in. He wanted to be back in the family circle, but his pride, his embarrassment, kept him out in the cold. He knew his parents had been trying to find him, but he just could not bring himself to say, "I'm sorry."

Upon hearing this story, I said to him, "Let's call them right now. I have an idea they will welcome you with open arms."

He was hesitant, but finally agreed and gave me the number. But as I began to dial, he got cold feet.

"Wait a minute," he said. "Let me think about it overnight." He told me he had a place to stay and that he would come back in the morning. When he left, I wondered if I would ever see him again.

Well, I did see him, but not in my office. I saw him that evening—hitchhiking—holding a sign that read New Orleans. I had a sad feeling deep down in my soul. Here was a young man running away from forgiveness, running away from a bright future, running away from his family—*trapped, paralyzed, shackled* in a prison of his own making, a prison constructed of pride and the fear of embarrassment.

I wonder how many people today are imprisoned like that. How many want to set something right? How many want to make a profession of faith for the first time, or ask for forgiveness, or make a new start. And yet, because of pride or fear of embarrassment, they turn away sorrowfully.

We can be trapped by our fear of rejection.

I heard about a young man who fell in love with a young woman. Even though he had heard that she liked him, too, he was insecure, unsure, afraid she might reject him. So he decided to try an unusual approach. Rather than call and ask her out, he would express his love from afar by writing a love letter every day for a full year. For 365 consecutive days, he wrote her a letter. Then at the end of the year, he finally got up the nerve to call and ask her out—only to discover that she had married the mailman!

Christ came to show us that we are not rejected. We are accepted! We don't need to be afraid. God reaches out to us with open arms. Fear of commitment, fear of embarrassment, fear of rejection, need not imprison us.

We can be trapped by our fear of God.

Jesus came to set us free from that fear. As I heard John Killinger once put it: "Jesus was God's way of getting rid of a bad reputation!" So often Jesus said, "Don't be afraid. Fear not. God is love."

A while back, I was visiting with a good friend. Her name is Julie and she is four years old. She was excited because she was going to see the movie *Snow White,* but a little nervous because she had heard about the wicked witch in the story.

But then she smiled and said with confidence, "It's O.K.! My father is going with me, and when the witch comes on, I won't look at the witch—I'll just look at my father!"

That is the good news of our faith! We don't need to be afraid. God is with us, and God is like a loving father! When we realize that, it sets us free. When we keep our eyes on him, we can meet life with strength, with confidence, with poise, and with love.

6

When You Face the Troubles of the World

John 16:25-33 "I have said this to you in figures; the hour is coming when I shall no longer speak to you in figures but tell you plainly of the Father. In that day you will ask in my name; and I do not say to you that I shall pray the Father for you; for the Father himself loves you, because you have loved me and have believed that I came from the Father. I came from the Father and have come into the world; again, I am leaving the world and going to the Father."

His disciples said, "Ah, now you are speaking plainly, not in any figure! Now we know that you know all things, and need none to question you; by this we believe that you came from God." Jesus answered them, "Do you now believe? The hour is coming, indeed it has come, when you will be scattered, every man to his home, and will leave me alone; yet I am not alone, for the Father is with me. I have said this to you, that in me you may have peace. In the world you have tribulation; but be of good cheer, I have overcome the world."

A schoolteacher once asked a group of children to write down on a card the one thing in the world they were most thankful for. Most of the children wrote down the usual, predictable things, but one little boy in the class said that he was most thankful for his glasses. The teacher was impressed. Some young people resent wearing eyeglasses, but here obviously was a young man mature enough to appreciate how glasses helped him.

"Johnny," she said, "I see that your glasses are the

thing for which you are most thankful. Is there any special reason?"

Johnny answered, "Yes, ma'am. My glasses keep the boys from hitting me and the girls from kissing me!" Now, Johnny had learned early that life can be tough—that we need all the help we can get.

One of the most delightful plays to hit Broadway in recent years was the popular musical *Annie,* which, of course, is based on the Little Orphan Annie comic strip.

At the beginning of the play, the little orphan girls sing "It's a Hard-knock Life!" We all can relate to that, can't we? We all have felt the painful hard knocks of life. Maybe that's why we so quickly empathize with the little girls trapped in Mrs. Hannigan's orphanage. If we use a little poetic license here (and a little imagination), we can see the story of Annie as a Christian allegory.

We discover a little orphan girl in a tough hard-knock life, wanting so much to be loved and to be saved from that desperate situation. Even though there seems no way out, she has *hope!* Notice that her hope is wrapped in the dream that someday her parents will come back to reclaim her. A lot of impostors (false prophets) come to claim her. Some even kidnap her, with the intention of destroying her. But finally she is rescued by the love and strength of Daddy Warbucks!

In this troubled world, we all have something of Annie in us. We want someone to help us, to reassure us, to deliver us. We want some word of "good news." We want someone to hold us up with love and strength and see us through. Well, that is precisely where the Christian faith comes in—and that is what the Christian faith is all about. Remember how Jesus said it: "In the world you have tribulation; but be of good cheer, I have overcome the world." In that dramatic pronouncement, three powerful phrases sum up the gospel. Let's look at those phrases.

In the world you have tribulation.

We quickly nod our heads in agreement. We don't need to be convinced. We know that we live in a troubled world. Read the front page of the newspaper any morning. Watch a news telecast any evening. The troubles of the world blare out at us, scream at us, cover us like a heavy blanket.

On the world scene there is the ever-present threat of nuclear war. There is always a crisis in the Middle East, and we hear rumblings in Central America. Across the face of the earth there are terrorist activities, bombings, kidnappings, revolutions, assassinations, riots. And there is hunger! And there is poverty!

On the national scene, we have seen Watergate and Contragate and Heavengate, and now there is AIDS, with its threats and problems and fears. We have seen scandals in government, scandals in labor, scandals in social life, scandals in college athletics, scandals in religion.

Albert Rasmussen has suggested that the way we spend our money is a clue to the things we love. He points out that in America, we spend more than three times as much for tobacco as for the entire religious enterprise; more than six times as much for liquor; nine times as much for automobiles; twice as much for movies.

Even the virtue of cleanliness seems to be losing out. A study showed that in the city of Cleveland there are now more television sets than bathtubs. People are better prepared to look at soap operas than to use soap!

On the local scene, we have been hit by a slumping economy. A friend of mine in the oil business has been having a tough time. When I called to check on him, he said, "I sleep like a baby. I sleep two hours and wake up and cry!"

And in our personal lives we know about troubles. We know about disappointment and disillusionment, hurt and heartache, pain and persecution, sorrow, sadness, and grief.

Well, how can the Christian faith help us? What does the Christian faith say to us as we live in this troubled world? That brings us to the second phrase:

But be of good cheer.

How absurd this must sound! Why would Jesus say that? Could he really be serious? Sure you have troubles, but be of good cheer. What does this mean? Does it mean we should be a Hail-fellow-well-met? Does it mean that if we walk about with a perpetual smile, act jolly, and laugh it up, our troubles will go away? Of course not! Certainly that is not what Jesus meant. (He himself was a "man of sorrows acquainted with grief.") What then does this phrase mean?

A glance back into the Greek New Testament helps us. We discover there that the Greek word *tharseite,* translated here "be of good cheer," may also be translated "be courageous!" In fact, the New English Bible accepts this as the best translation and renders it like this:

"In the world, you will have trouble. But courage!" Take courage! So to be of good cheer means to be courageous in the living of these days. Now, there is a reason—a special reason—we can be courageous in the face of the troubles of the world. And that brings us to the third and final phrase:

For Christ has overcome the world!

Now, do we believe this? I mean, does it really have meaning for us? Or is it just a clever cliché we can quote when we can't think of anything else to say? Has Christ really overcome the world? The biblical answer, the Christian answer, is an emphatic and dramatic *Yes!* Some years ago I heard a powerful parable of the Last Judgment, which makes the point extremely well.

At the end of time, all the people who had ever lived were brought before the throne of God to be judged. However, they were not a submissive crowd. They were mumbling and grumbling among themselves. They had complaints to make.

One group was made up of Jews who had suffered great persecution. Some had died in gas chambers and concentration camps. How could God judge them? What could he know of their suffering? "Who is God, that he should be our judge?" they cried.

Then there was a group of slaves who had suffered all kinds of indignities. There were homeless people who had no place to lay their heads. And there were poor folks—workers who had never been able to make ends meet. There were sick ones and sufferers of all kinds, each with a complaint against God!

"How could God judge us?" they thought. How lucky

God is, to live in heaven where all is goodness and light—no tears, no worries, no fears, no hunger, no inhumanities.

So a commission was appointed to draw up the case against God! It was simple. Their conclusion was that before God could judge them, he must first endure what they had endured. So they judged God, and they sentenced him to live on earth as a man, to submit to the painful, agonizing, troublesome hard knocks of life. They shouted out:

> Let him be born a Jew!
> Let him be born poor!
> Give him hard work to do!
> Let him be rejected by his people!
> Give him for friends only those who are held in contempt!
> Let him be betrayed by one of his friends!
> Let him be indicted on false charges, tried before a prejudiced jury, and convicted by a cowardly judge!
> Let him be abandoned by his friends!
> Let him be tortured!
> Let him be lonely!
> Let him die at the hands of his enemies!

As each group announced its sentence to God, cheers of approval went up from the throng. Then suddenly, there was quiet. No one moved. No one uttered a word or made a sound. For everyone knew that God already had served that sentence!

That is why we can be courageous. That is why we need not be afraid. That is why we can face the troubles of this world with strength and confidence. We can trust in God because God speaks not from an easy chair, but from a cross—as one who endured the worst the world can do and was victorious!

That's what the cross means. God wins! God's goodness cannot be defeated. God's truth cannot be silenced. Ultimately God wins, and he wants to share that victory with us. In the world we will have troubles, but we can be courageous. For Christ suffered the worst this world can dish out, and he overcame it. And he wants to share with us the Victor's crown!

7

When You Must Choose to Be Self-centered or Self-giving

Luke 15:11-24 And he said, "There was a man who had two sons; and the younger of them said to his father, 'Father, give me the share of property that falls to me.' And he divided his living between them. Not many days later, the younger son gathered all he had and took his journey into a far country, and there he squandered his property in loose living. And when he had spent everything, a great famine arose in that country, and he began to be in want. So he went and joined himself to one of the citizens of that country, who sent him into his fields to feed swine. And he would gladly have fed on the pods that the swine ate; and no one gave him anything. But when he came to himself he said, 'How many of my father's hired servants have bread enough and to spare, but I perish here with hunger! I will arise and go to my father, and I will say to him, "Father, I have sinned against heaven and before you; I am no longer worthy to be called your son; treat me as one of your hired servants."' And he arose and came to his father. But while he was yet at a distance, his father saw him and had compassion, and ran and embraced him and kissed him. And the son said to him, 'Father, I have sinned against heaven and before you; I am no longer worthy to be called your son.' But the father said to his servants, 'Bring quickly the best robe, and put it on him; and put a ring on his hand, and shoes on his feet; and bring the fatted calf and kill it, and let us eat and make merry; for this my son was dead, and is alive again; he was lost, and is found.' And they began to make merry."

Rodney Wilmouth, a friend of mine, told a story that touched me greatly. Let me share it with you.

Some years ago a Chinese artist, a new Christian, wanted to paint the parable of the prodigal son. His first attempt showed the prodigal son far down the road, coming toward home. The father was standing at the front gate, his arms folded across his chest, looking sternly down the road with an "I told you so" expression.

When the artist showed the painting to a friend, the friend said, "Technically, it's a beautiful work of art, but it misses the point of the parable! The father should not be standing and waiting. He should not be looking sternly at the prodigal. He should be running to meet his son! He is overjoyed to see him alive and well. He can't wait to receive him, to forgive him, to hug him, to welcome him home!"

"But most fathers could not do that," said the artist.

"That may be true," said the friend, "but this parable was told by Jesus to show us what God is like—to show dramatically his gracious, unconditional love, his eagerness to set things right, his quickness to forgive."

"I see," replied the artist.

So he painted another picture and again called his friend to come to see it. This time the father is shown running excitedly toward the prodigal, his robes flapping in the wind, a look of joy on his face. But interestingly, the father's shoes are two different colors—they don't match!

The friend complimented the artist on the painting, then added, "I must ask you about the father's shoes. They don't match. Why?"

The artist answered, "Because the father is so overjoyed to see his son coming home that he grabs the two nearest shoes and puts them on and runs to meet him. He doesn't care that the shoes don't match. All that matters is that his son was lost and now he is found. The father represents our God, who is so anxious to get on with the forgiving and the love and the celebration, that it doesn't matter that his shoes don't match!"

Isn't that a great story? "The God whose shoes don't match"—a perceptive depiction of what the prodigal son parable is all about. But this magnificent parable shows us not only what God is like, it also shows us what he wants us to be like. He wants us to live in that gracious spirit! He wants us to be anxious to love, quick to forgive, eager to reconcile.

When we read the second half of the parable, this becomes clear, because while the father is gracious and forgiving, we see a different story with the elder brother. He is angry, resentful, critical, frustrated. The father rushes out to encourage him to forgive and come to the homecoming dinner. But there is no forgiveness in the elder brother, no compassion, no celebration, no unmatched shoes here. Bitterly, he turns away—and he misses the party.

The point is clear: God is like that father. He is loving, merciful, compassionate, and quick to forgive—and he wants us to live in that spirit. And when we live in that spirit, life is celebrative. When we don't, we become likely prospects for a life of bitterness, misery, and loneliness. In the church, in our families, and in our personal relationships, we can live in that spirit.

In the Church—
we can live in that gracious spirit.

We can be a church whose shoes don't match—quick to be gracious, quick to accept people, eager to reconcile, anxious to love, willing to love unconditionally.

One of the finest professors of preaching in America today is Fred Craddock. I heard him speak about his father. When Fred Craddock was growing up, his father didn't go to church. He would stay at home, complaining about the hypocrites, grumbling and fussing about dinner being late on Sunday. Once in a while the pastor would come and try to talk to him, but he was kind of rough on the minister.

"I know about you folks down at the church," he would say. "You aren't really interested in me. All you fellows want is another name on your rolls and another pledge for your budget."

Fred Craddock's mother, who loved the church deeply, was so embarrassed when her husband talked to the minister like that, she would go into the kitchen and cry.

Every new pastor would try his best to win Mr. Craddock over, to no avail. Sometimes a guest evangelist would come to the church, and the pastor would say, "Here's the toughie! See him!"

And Mr. Craddock would tell them again: "You don't care about me. All you want is a new name for your rolls and a new pledge for your budget!"

But one time he didn't say it. He was in the Veterans Hospital, and Fred Craddock rushed across the country to see him. They had operated, but they said it was too late. They had inserted a tube so that he could breathe, but he couldn't speak.

As Fred Craddock looked around the room, he saw gifts of love everywhere—beautiful cut flowers, potted plants, thoughtful gifts, cards, and letters—from Men's Bible Class, Women's Study Class, Youth Fellowship.

And every single one of them was from persons or groups connected with the church!

When Fred Craddock's father saw him looking at the gifts, he took a pencil and wrote on the side of the tissue box a line from *Hamlet:* "In this harsh world, draw your breath in pain to tell my story."

Fred Craddock looked at what his father had written. Then he asked, "What is your story, Dad?"

His father took the pencil again and wrote, "Tell them I was wrong!"

Rebuffed time and again, that church did the right thing—they kept on loving! They were quick to be there. They loved graciously and unconditionally. Their shoes didn't match. Every church should live in that spirit.

> *In our families—*
> *we can live in that gracious spirit.*

Some years ago, I held a funeral for a young man who had died suddenly in his mid-thirties, leaving his wife and a young daughter. The week before his death, he had given a special birthday present to his daughter—a coin collection he had kept since he was eight years old. It was not worth a lot materially; it was a sentimental gift which he wanted to pass on to his daughter on her eighth birthday.

Three days after the funeral, when the wife and daughter were visiting with the man's mother, the little girl told her grandmother about the coin collection. The grandmother abruptly told them to return the coin collection to her. She wanted it.

When they explained that he had given the collection to his daughter for her birthday, the grandmother told them to get out of her house; that if they didn't bring the coin collection back to her soon, she would never speak to them again. The wife and daughter left, crying.

The next day, the man's mother told me what had happened and asked what I would do if I were she.

I realized that this was an emotional situation for her, so I measured my words: "Now, of course, it's your decision, but if you really want to know what I would do, I'll tell you. You know, you could lose your granddaughter over this, and I don't think it's worth that. So if I were you, I would go to them immediately and say, 'I'm sorry. We are all hurting in this awful grief experience, and I haven't been myself since my son's death. I was upset yesterday, and I didn't mean those things I said. Of course I want my granddaughter to have the coin collection. That's what he would want. I'm so sorry. Please forgive me!' That's what I would do."

She looked at me with tough eyes and said sternly, "All hell will freeze over before I would do that!"

Her granddaughter is eighteen now. She graduated from high school last spring and is now in college. Her grandmother has not seen her or spoken to her for more than ten years.

Isn't that sad? Isn't that tragic? In our families, we need shoes that don't match. We need to be quick to reconcile, anxious to love and forgive, eager to set things right.

In our personal relationships—
we can live in that gracious spirit.

The noted English poet George Herbert was a member of a small group of friends who periodically met to play musical instruments. One night on the way to a meeting of the group, Herbert passed a man whose cart was stuck in a muddy ditch. He immediately put his instrument aside and went to help. When the cart was finally out of the mud, George Herbert was covered with sticky clay. When he arrived at the meeting, he apologized for his tardiness and his muddy appearance.

They said, "George, you have missed all the music!"

George Herbert only smiled and said, "Yes, but I will have songs at midnight!"

When we are quick to help someone who is hurting, quick to care for others unconditionally, quick to serve rather than sentence, quick to love rather than lecture, quick to console rather than condemn, quick to forgive rather than demand our pound of flesh—then we can have songs at midnight and shoes that do not match, because we are living in God's gracious spirit.

In a Peanuts story, Lucy has had an argument with her mother and Charlie Brown is trying to help.

He says: "Lucy, go to her and say, 'I'm sorry, dear mother. I'm sorry. Please forgive me.' Now, let me hear you say that."

Lucy tries it: "I'm sorry, dear mother. I'm sorry. Please for—" Then she clenches her fist and screams, "I'd rather die!"

Well, that is precisely what we must do. We must die to selfish, arrogant pride before we can be resurrected to grace, to life, to compassion, to God's magnificent unmatched shoes—a forgiving spirit! We must die to selfishness before we can come alive to love!

8

When Your Self-esteem Is Low

Luke 10:25-28 And behold, a lawyer stood up to put him to the test, saying, "Teacher, what shall I do to inherit eternal life?" He said to him, "What is written in the law? How do you read?" And he answered, "You shall love the Lord your God with all your heart, and with all your soul, and with all your strength, and with all your mind; and your neighbor as yourself." And he said to him, "You have answered right; do this, and you will live."

In the church, we talk a lot about *love*. We teach it, we preach it, we sing about it, we try to live it—and well we should, because love is the message of the church and the dominant theme of the scriptures. *Love* is the Christian faith summed up in one word! Jesus called it the sign of discipleship.

Usually when we talk about love, we lift up love for God and love for others, and that is well and good. But I want to turn the coin over and raise what I think is a very important question: Is it O.K. to love yourself? How can you love yourself without being selfish or arrogant or getting caught up in the epidemic of me-ism?

As a backdrop to our thinking, read again that verse above from Luke 10. *"Love God with all your heart, soul, mind and strength . . . and love your neighbor as you love yourself."* In this important section of Scripture, three kinds of love are spelled out—two directly and one implied—love for God, love for neighbor, and love for self. Jesus instructs us to love God and neighbor, and he implies that it's O.K. to love yourself.

Now I want us to think about that implication, because over the years, I have become increasingly convinced that not only it is O.K. to love yourself, but it is tremendously important. Proper self-love—positive self-esteem—is essential to health and happiness and wholeness!

Some months ago, I had just finished a wedding rehearsal and had come back to my office to clear off my desk before leaving for home. The church was empty and dark and quiet. Then I heard a knock at the door. When I responded, I found a well-dressed young man who looked to be in his mid-thirties. I found out later that he was an attorney. His face was pale and drained. Fear and panic were in his eyes. I invited him in and we introduced ourselves.

He sat down and started to talk: "I need your prayers. I feel so terribly alone, so confused and mixed up. I can't seem to pray to God for myself, and I have no friends anymore. I came here tonight with the thought of ending it all, but then I saw the steeple of your church. That stopped me, and I thought there might be some help here for my loneliness."

I told him our church would like to help him, and I asked if he could tell me more about what was troubling him.

He said, *"Everything's gone wrong.* I have lost confidence in my professional ability, my wife has left me, I can't get along with my children, I'm cut off from my parents and my in-laws, I'm having conflicts with my co-workers, I've been drinking heavily. Everybody has left me, and I don't blame them. I've been bitter and hostile. I've done so many mean and cruel things . . . and now I have so many problems." He paused and took a deep breath.

Then he leaned forward and said, "To tell you the truth, I think all those problems are really symptoms. My real problem is that I don't like myself—and that taints everything I touch and do!"

Well, he was probably right. When you don't feel good about yourself, it smudges and distorts every relationship. As I listened to that young lawyer, I remembered something that psychologists and psychiatrists are saying more and more these days. Whenever we encounter a person who is constantly bitter, continually critical, always complaining, perpetually finding fault, and repeatedly saying cruel things that wound the hearts of friends, we can be sure we are dealing with someone who does not like himself or herself. That seething, brooding bitterness is merely a projection of his or her own self-contempt.

- Think of the *alcoholic* who despises himself and what he is becoming, who loathes his inability to cope with his problem, who wrestles constantly with guilt, and as a result is mean to his wife and children.

- Think of the *college student* who doesn't study, flunks her exam—then, disgusted with herself, lashes out at her roommate with hostile, critical words.

- Think of the *business executive* who misses out on the big deal, loses it—then, aggravated with himself, blasts his family with a temper tantrum and kicks the dog.

We all have experienced this, haven't we? The key is to recognize it when it happens and expose it. Then we can handle it better. Let's be honest. Isn't it usually true that when we fuss at someone, it's really because we are upset with ourselves?

Ernest Fitzgerald once told of having a bad day. He had mishandled some things, and he came home frustrated and angry with himself. Now, it so happened that his wife had bought him a new suit that day. He tried it on and began to complain bitterly.

"I can't believe you bought this suit. It looks horrible. The color is wrong. The style is wrong. It doesn't fit."

"O.K.! O.K.!" his wife responded. "I'll take it back!"

The next day was a great day for Bishop Fitzgerald. He accomplished a lot, corrected some of his mistakes of the day before, and came home feeling good about himself and about life. When he went into the bedroom, he immediately saw a suit hanging on his closet door, and he thought his wife had exchanged the other suit for this one. He tried it on.

"Now, this is more like it. This suit looks good. It feels good and it fits great. It's perfect," he said to his wife.

To which she responded, "Ernest, that is the same suit you tried on yesterday!"

When we are unhappy with ourselves, we project that aggravation onto other people. On the other hand, when we feel good about ourselves, we are more loving, patient, kind, and gracious toward everyone we see. Many of our deep personal problems arise from a lack of proper self-love. Many of the sins we commit, wrongs we do, crutches we lean on, irritations we experience—

these come from not feeling good about ourselves. It's what Transactional Analysis calls feeling not O.K. How important it is that we have a healthy sense of self-esteem! In "Myself," Edgar Guest put it like this:

> I have to live with myself, and so
> I want to be fit for myself to know;
> I want to be able, as days go by,
> Always to look myself straight in the eye;
> I don't want to stand, with the setting sun,
> And hate myself for the things I've done.
>
> I don't want to keep on a closet shelf,
> A lot of secrets about myself,
> And fool myself, as I come and go,
> Into thinking that nobody else will know. . . .
>
> I know what others may never know;
> I never can fool myself, and so,
> Whatever happens, I want to be
> Self-respecting and conscience free.

Self-respect is so important! A healthy self-love is essential to a productive, creative, meaningful life. Self-hatred is destructive and dangerous; low self-esteem is crippling. There can be several bad consequences of disliking ourselves.

Disliking ourselves can lead to bitterness.

And bitterness can cause us to be critical of everything and hostile toward everyone. Psychologists have told us repeatedly that those who are at war with themselves will constantly be at war with others. Only when we like ourselves can we reach out meaningfully to other people.

Disliking ourselves can lead to insecurity.

And insecurity can cause us to worry, fret, run scared, and be anxiety-ridden, suspicious of everyone and everything. Some people are so insecure that they can turn compliments into insults.

For example, I remember the time I said to someone, "My, my! Don't you look nice today!"

Quick as a flash the woman retorted, "You said 'today'! I guess that means you think I usually don't look nice!"

That kind of insecurity is destructive and depleting. It robs us of the joy of life—and makes everybody uncomfortable.

Disliking ourselves can lead to jealousy.

And jealousy can cause us to be envious, resentful, sometimes even cruel. When you don't like yourself, you see every other person as a rival, an enemy, someone who has it better than you, someone you have to put down or undercut.

A couple of years ago, a woman wanted me to arrange for her to see a psychiatrist.

She said, "I have a real problem that is getting out of hand. I am extremely jealous. I resent the good fortune of my friends, and I'm so suspicious of my husband that I'm afraid I may fly into a rage and cause someone to get hurt."

I referred her to a psychiatrist, and after one session he called me.

"I know her problem," he said. "She doesn't like herself, and she can't like or love anyone else until she learns how to feel good about herself." Self-hate is dangerous. It can lead to volatile jealously and cause us to hurt other people, even those closest to us.

Disliking ourselves can lead to guilt.

And guilt can cause us to look for scapegoats, someone to blame it on. Like Adam and Eve, who pointed the accusing finger at each other and at the serpent, many people today feel guilty because they don't like themselves. Since they can't stand the burden of their guilt feelings, they indicate to whoever walks by, "There's nothing wrong with me! *You* are the one! It's all *your* fault!" They point at others, hoping no one will look at them.

Disliking ourselves can lead to self-pity.

Remember how Charlie Brown put it: "The whole world hates me." This kind of self-pity causes us to look for crutches—temporary pick-me-ups like drugs or alcohol—which only add to the problem. They don't pick us up; they let us down. They don't make us stronger; they make us weaker.

Do you want to feel good about yourself? Do you want to like yourself more? Then *remember this:* You are special to God! You are valuable to him. You are a child of God, and nothing can cut you off from him and his love. You are a unique partner with God.

A teacher once asked on a quiz, "What is in the world now that was not here fifty years ago?"

One little girl wrote simply—me! and she was right.

You and I are unique in the world. You and I are new and different from anything this world has ever seen. You and I have something unique to do, something unique to offer and give and be. We can't all be Schweitzers or Carvers or Wesleys or Mother Teresas or Pauls, but all God wants is that we use what we have, do what we can do, become what we can become. In your corner of the world, there awaits a special task, a unique work which only you can do. You are special to God!

If you ever doubt that or wonder about it, remember the story about the old man who was brought to a hospital emergency room late one evening, an apparent heart-attack victim. He was ill-clothed and disheveled and appeared to be unconscious.

One of the young medical students took one look at him and said, "What in the world should we do with this worthless wretch?"

The old man opened his eyes slightly and in an amazingly strong voice said, *"Call him not worthless for whom Christ died!"*

9

When Your Foundation Is Shaky

Matthew 7:24-29 "Every one then who hears these words of mine and does them will be like a wise man who built his house upon the rock; and the rain fell, and the floods came, and the winds blew and beat upon that house, but it did not fall, because it had been founded on the rock. And every one who hears these words of mine and does not do them will be like a foolish man who built his house upon the sand; and the rain fell, and the floods came, and the winds blew and beat against that house, and it fell; and great was the fall of it."

And when Jesus finished these sayings, the crowds were astonished at his teaching, for he taught them as one who had authority, and not as their scribes.

O n our vacation one summer we spent some time at Land Between the Lakes in Kentucky. One evening, we drove over to Paducah to see an incredible performance by one of the living legends of show business, Red Skelton. Approaching eighty years of age, he was still as bright, sharp, talented, and as funny as ever. He told a true story that I would like to share with you.

A secretary on his staff had done some extra work for him, and he wanted to buy her a nice gift to express his appreciation. He asked his wife what would be an appropriate gift.

Mrs. Skelton suggested perfume and encouraged

him to tell the secretary ahead of time what he planned to buy and find out if she had a favorite fragrance.

The secretary very humbly replied, *"Oh Mr. Skelton, I love working for you. You don't have to buy me a gift."*

But Red persisted and the young secretary finally said, "Well, if you insist, my favorite perfume is called Romantic Thoughts at Midnight."

With that information, Red Skelton went to a nearby department store and made his way to the perfume department, where an older woman stood behind the counter.

Red Skelton said to her, "Pardon me, but do you have Romantic Thoughts at Midnight?"

The clerk answered, "Listen, Sonny, I have to drink coffee to stay up for the ten o'clock news!"

Well, obviously they had a communication problem. Oh, what problems we do have with communication! Oh, how we mis-hear and misunderstand and misquote one another! We say something we think is perfectly clear, only to discover later that someone heard it in a totally different way. What the person heard was completely different from what we meant.

Jesus was very much aware of these kinds of problems, so he quite often illustrated his message with a story or parable. *When he wanted to show what God is like,* he told the powerful parable of the prodigal son. And he revealed there, clearly and dramatically, that God is like a loving parent. *When he wanted to expose the sin of apathy,* he told the poignant parable of the talents. And there he revealed graphically that if we don't use our abilities, we lose them. *When he wanted to remind us that every person we meet is our neighbor,* he told the unforgettable parable of the good Samaritan. There he revealed plainly that we should love and care for all people, especially those in trouble.

Well, here we see him at it again. At the end of Matthew 7, Jesus is communicating a great truth with a picturesque story. Actually, this is the conclusion of his Sermon on the Mount, and he is driving home the message with this parable about building our lives on a firm foundation.

Throughout the Sermon (recorded in Matthew 5, 6, and 7), Jesus has been saying that it is not enough to play at religion, not enough to talk a good game, not enough to just go through the motions. That kind of shallowness and shakiness will not hold us up when the storms lash us. The Christian life must be built on a firm, solid, dependable foundation, or life's stormy times will tear us apart.

In the Sermon on the Mount, Jesus outlines the key qualities of the Christian life-style in what we now refer to as the Beatitudes. He lifts up such special qualities as humility, mercy, peace-making, and purity. Next he calls for us to be winsome in our witness, single-minded in our devotion, unconditional in our loving, genuine in our religious practices, humble in our piety, unflinching in our trust, productive in our goodness.

And then he ends the sermon with the candid parable about the wise man who builds his house (i.e., his life) on a rock and the foolish man who builds his house (or his life) on sand. Now this parable, coming where it does, becomes even more powerful as we recognize its implication—that what Jesus has just said in the sermon is the real foundation for life as God intended it! And if you and I build our lives on those things, we can know a full life, and we can withstand any storm that may come. Anything less is shaky sand that will not hold us up.

Now let's expose some of these "shaky sands." Jesus uncovered three of them in the Sermon on the Mount: *self-centeredness, resentment,* and *fear*—all poor foundations for life.

The Sand of Self-centeredness

Again and again in the Sermon, Jesus denounces self-centeredness as an enemy of life, a poor foundation, a shaky sand. Remember his strong words: No one can serve two masters. . . . You cannot serve God and mammon. . . . Do not lay up treasures on earth, where moth and rust consume and thieves break in and steal. . . . Seek first God's kingdom and his righteousness. . . . Don't be hypocrites. . . . Don't show off. . . . Don't act pious. . . . Be humble-minded!

The Bible, from cover to cover, is emphatic about this—self-centeredness will ultimately destroy us. Never before in history has this been more true. John Donne was right: "No man is an island." We are all in this together. Telecommunication, mass media, and modern travel have made our world a global village. A President's sneeze in Washington can affect the economy in Japan.

I heard a story recently that makes the point. Two men were sitting together on a plane, cruising high above the clouds, when suddenly one of them exclaimed, "Look at that! The right engine is on fire!"

The other man replied, "Aren't we lucky to be sitting on the left side!"

But if the plane goes down, both sides will go down.

We live in one rapidly shrinking world; never before have we been so closely related and interdependent. When will we learn to see others not as enemies, but as neighbors? We are all on the same plane. Self-centeredness won't do. Self-centeredness takes us back to the jungle. As someone once said, "If we don't learn how to live together soon, we will all be *cremated* equal!

I once saw a painting in which the artist depicts an old Chinese legend about heaven and hell. On one side of the painting, hell is portrayed. It shows a group of people seated at a great table with a sumptuous feast before them. But the people are miserable. They can't eat the magnificent feast because their chopsticks are longer than their arms. They can't get the food to their mouths. So they sit there starving, their faces drawn with hunger and self-pity.

Next to that picture is a picture of heaven. It depicts the same people, the same banquet, the same long chopsticks. There is only one subtle and significant difference. The people in the heaven picture are radiantly happy. Their faces are vibrant with joy because they are *feeding each other!* They are reaching across the table with the long chopsticks and feeding the persons seated across from them.

The point of this ancient legend is precisely the point I want to make—the difference between heaven and hell is self-centeredness. Hell is symbolized by self-centeredness and self-pity, heaven is symbolized by self-giving and sharing. Self-centeredness is shaky sand—a poor foundation for these stormy times. But self-giving love is a rock—a firm foundation for the living of these days. So let the storms rage, let the rains fall, let the winds blow and beat upon our house. It will not fall if it is built on self-giving.

The Sand of Resentment

Again and again in the Sermon on the Mount, Jesus denounces resentment as an enemy of life, a weak foundation, a shaky sand that will hold us up. Remember what he said: Judge not. . . . Love your enemies. . . . Pray for those who persecute you. . . . Go and be reconciled. . . . Be merciful. . . . Be peace-makers. . . . Don't be resentful. . . . Go the second mile. . . . The Scriptures make it clear that the key sign of discipleship is love. To put on Christ is to put on love. It is to see all people with "Christed eyes," as persons of integrity and worth, as brothers and sisters, as children of God. Therefore resentment doesn't work. It is an enemy of life. Resentment, anger, jealousy, envy, vengeance, hate—whatever you want to call it—that destructive spirit is a poor foundation for life. It is a shaky sand that will not hold us up.

I recently read a story about a twelve-year-old boy who was in trouble at school. He had no friends and was unhappy and resentful. But he had noticed a dramatic change in his dad, so he asked him about it.

The father said, "Well, son, I was making a big mess of my life, and I decided I'd ask God to take it over and show me how to live it. And it has made all the difference."

The boy thought a moment. Then he said, "Dad, I think I'd like to do that too."

Two weeks later, when the father returned from a business trip, his son met him at the airport with the news: "Dad, do you know what God has done? He's changed every kid in my class!"

Well, God does indeed change people. He also opens our eyes so that we can look at them differently. God can change the eyes of resentment to the eyes of love. Resentment is shaky sand. But love is a *rock*, a great foundation on which to build our lives. So let the storms rage, let the rains fall, let the winds blow and beat upon the house—it will not fall if it's built on love.

The Sand of Fear

In the Sermon on the Mount, time and again Jesus exposes fear, anxiety, fretfulness, needless worry, as shaky sands that cannot hold us up. Remember his words: *Do not fear. . . . Do not be anxious. . . . Don't worry. . . . Don't fret. . . . Be at peace. . . . Trust God. . . . He will never desert you. . . . God will see you through.*

In "Overheard in an Orchard," Elizabeth Cheney expressed it like this:

> Said the Robin to the Sparrow:
> "I should really like to know
> Why these anxious human beings
> Rush about and worry so."
>
> Said the Sparrow the Robin:
> "Friend, I think that it must be
> That they have no heavenly father,
> Such as cares for you and me."

We don't need to run scared—God is for us. God is with us. He will see us through any storm. Self-centeredness, resentment, fear—these are weak foundations for our lives. They are shifting, shaky sands that will not hold us up. But if we build our lives on self-giving and love and unshakable trust in God, we can withstand any storm.

Isn't that what conversion is? Christ comes into our lives and changes our self-centeredness to self-giving, our resentment to love, our fear to a confident trust in God! So let the storms rage, let the rains fall, let the winds blow. We will be ready for anything, for Christ is our solid Rock!

10

When It Comes to Forgiveness

Matthew 18:21-22 Then Peter came up and said to him, "Lord, how often shall my brother sin against me, and I forgive him? As many as seven times?" Jesus said to him, "I do not say to you seven times, but seventy times seven."

The picture was of two men shaking hands—two very different men from radically different worlds. One man was young, the other older; one a Muslim, the other a Christian; one in a resplendent white robe, the other in the drab garb of a prisoner; one a beloved and respected world leader, the other a convicted criminal. Two years before, one of these men had tried to kill the other. The picture on the cover of *Time* magazine, January 9, 1984, led to the story inside:

In a bare, white-walled cell in Rome's Rebibbia prison, John Paul tenderly held the hand that had held the gun that was meant to kill him. For 21 minutes, the Pope sat with his would-be assassin, Mehmet Ali Agca. The two talked softly. Once or twice, Agca laughed. The Pope forgave him for the shooting. At the end of the meeting, Agca either kissed the Pope's ring or pressed the Pope's hand to his forehead in a Muslim gesture of respect.

What Pope John Paul did there in Rebibbia prison was profoundly Christian! He sought out the enemy, embraced the enemy, and forgave him. The caption read, "Does forgiveness have a place in an age of violence and vengeance?" The answer to that is indeed a resounding *Yes!* And that is the message John Paul was sending to the world. That is the message he was sending to Iran and Israel, to Russia and America, and to you and to me.

All during 1983, the Pope had preached reconciliation. Now, with his gracious visit to Agca, he was acting it out, dramatizing his message.

I'm sure Pope John Paul has done many good things in his lifetime, but none could be more Christ-like! I'm sure he has preached many great sermons, but none could be more eloquent! I'm sure he has performed many kind deeds, but none could have been more timely!

At Rebibbia prison, he shouted out to the world: "Violence is unacceptable as a solution to our problems. Violence is unworthy of man. Violence is a lie, for it goes against the truth of our faith, the truth of our humanity."

The scene in that prison cell—the image of Pope John Paul seeking out the man who had made a violent attempt on his life, that picture of forgiveness—shines brightly in dramatic contrast to what the world sees on the evening news. Those programs are filled with stories of vengeance and violence, bloodshed and threats, wars and rumors of war. But there in that little white-walled cell, one man reminded us of something very important: We don't need to be bitter, or angry, or resentful, or hostile; we can respond, even to inhuman acts, by being sane, civilized, humane, forbearing, and Christian.

The Pope obviously thought of this meeting as an example to the world of the healing power of forgiveness! Think about it. If John Paul could forgive his would-be assassin, why couldn't other world leaders sit down together and come to some kind of reconciliation?

Now, I know how the world looks at forgiveness. We like it, but we are a little suspicious. We are touched when it happens, but it makes us nervous. We tend to lean toward cold, hard power, the way of the avenger, looking out for our own rights and demanding retribution. Forgiveness is nice, we think, but it smacks of weakness. Forgiveness does not look much like a tool for survival in a violent world. But that is exactly what it is. It is our *only hope* for survival!

Oh, how I wish we could grow up and learn this basic fact of life. Oh, how I wish we could learn this dependable spiritual law—that it's O.K. to forgive. Indeed, it's beautiful to forgive. It's a sign of *strength,* not weakness.

I read Larry McMurtry's *Terms of Endearment* again just to get the feel of what it's about. I came to that powerful scene when young Tommy and his mother, Emma, who have not been getting along well, are saying good-bye. Emma is dying, and the boy is tense and awkward as he hugs her. She says to him,

> Tommy, be sweet. . . . Don't keep pretending you don't like me. . . . I love you more than anybody in the world . . . and I'm not going to be around long enough to change my mind about you. . . . In a year or two when I'm not around to irritate you you're going to change your mind and

remember that I read you a lot of stories and made you a lot of milkshakes. . . . You're going to remember that you love me. . . . You'll wish you could tell me that you've changed your mind, but you won't be able to, so I'm telling you now I already know you love me, just so you won't be in doubt about that later.

Who is the strong one here? Not the one who tries to act strong and macho, but Emma, the dying mother, who reaches out with love and understanding, mercy, compassion, empathy, and forgiveness, to try in her own way to protect her son from feelings of guilt, which she knows are sure to come. Forgiveness is not weakness! Forgiveness requires great, great strength!

When will we learn? We spend weary days and sleepless nights brooding over our resentments, calculating ways to get even. We demand our pound of flesh, seeth over our grievances, and wallow in our self-pity, shackled by our silly pride—unbending, unmerciful, unable and unwilling to forgive. Isn't that tragic?

A cruel word is finally only an echo. Revenge actually is never sweet; it ultimately becomes a sour stomach and a bitter mercy. Violence breeds more violence. Hate poisons the soul! Jesus knew this, and he called on us to be *bridge builders,* to be *peacemakers,* to seek *forgiveness* and to offer it. How we need the spirit of forgiveness in our world today!

There is a story about a man who was in terrible physical condition. He was tired, weak.

He said to his doctor, "Tell me what to do. I feel drained and exhausted. I have this chronic headache, and I feel worn out all the time. What's the best thing I can do?"

The doctor, knowing the man's wild life-style said, "I'll tell you exactly what to do. Each day after work, go home and get a good night's rest. Stop drinking, stop carousing, stop running around all night. That's the best thing you can do."

The man was silent a moment. Then he asked, "What's the *next* best thing?"

We might as well admit it. Broken relationships, hostility, and violence blight our world. They reduce the meaning of life for everyone involved. Forgiveness is the answer, and we know that; yet we continue to ask, "What's the *next* best thing I can do?" In a way, we are a bundle of contradictions. On the one hand, we need one another, and I think most people really want to get along with others. But then communication falters. Suspicion creeps in, and we end up misunderstanding and hurting and frustrating one another.

Resentment, anger, jealousy, fear, selfishness—these things poison us. And we say and do things that separate people and break hearts. Or we treat one another with cold indifference and remain remote and inaccessible.

And that is why much of Jesus' teaching centers on forgiveness. He knew that no love, no marriage, no friendship, no family, no church, no society, no world can live without it. How we need the spirit of forgiveness in our world today!

This was a key theme of many of Jesus' parables. This was a dominant theme in his Sermon on the Mount. This was the major theme of his life. And this is why the visit of Pope John Paul II to Rebibbia prison was so profoundly Christian.

In Matthew's Gospel, chapter 18, Simon Peter asks

Jesus, "How often shall I forgive my brother?" Of course, Simon knew the Jewish law: Forgive a first offense, forgive a second and a third, but punish the fourth—forgive three times, but then get even!

Simon Peter, wanting to show his magnanimous spirit (and perhaps hoping to impress Jesus) went beyond the Talmud: "Shall I forgive him seven times?"

But Christ's teaching is that forgiveness should be *unlimited*: "No, not 7 times, but 70 times 7!" And by that Jesus means, forgive every time! Forgive an untold, never-ending number of times.

For the Jews, the number seven was the number of perfection. When time has run through seven days, it begins again; the cycle is complete. So no expression could more forcibly convey the fact that forgiveness is to be unlimited than this—"Forgive 70 times 7."

Forgiveness is not a matter of arithmetic, anyway. It's not a matter of asking, "How many times must I hold off before I hit back?" No, forgiveness is an overflowing spirit. It keeps no score of wrongs; it holds no grudges. It is merciful, as *God* is merciful!

"Should I forgive that person who has wronged me or hurt me?" If that question ever comes to your mind, remember the picture of Christ hanging on a cross, saying, *"Father, forgive them!"* That is our measuring stick. That's the inspiration of Christian forgiveness.

To be Christian is to be Christ-like; it is to have *his* gracious and forgiving ways!

One quick footnote: Agca is forgiven by the Pope, but he is still in prison. The point is that forgiveness is always available to us, but sometimes even when forgiveness comes, we must live with the consequences of our wrongdoing.

But as far as we are concerned, the real message is what Pope John Paul was trying to say to the world: "Forgiveness is the answer—not violence, not vengeance, not resentment, not hatred, but forgiveness! We are called to be forgivers!"

A few weeks ago, a good friend of mine who happens to be nine years old shared with me something very special—*Where the Sidewalk Ends*, a book of poems and drawings by Shel Silverstein. One brief poem is called

HUG O' WAR

I will not play at tug o' war.
I'd rather play at hug o' war,
Where everyone hugs
Instead of tugs,
Where everyone giggles
And rolls on the rug,
Where everyone kisses,
And everyone grins,
And everyone cuddles,
And everyone wins.

When it comes to forgiveness, we have a choice. We can tug, or we can hug; we can get bitter, or we can get better.

11

When the Church Cries for Help

I Corinthians 12:1-11 Now concerning spiritual gifts, brethren, I do not want you to be uninformed. You know that when you were heathen, you were led astray to dumb idols, however you may have been moved. Therefore I want you to understand that no one speaking by the Spirit of God ever says "Jesus be cursed!" and no one can say "Jesus is Lord" except by the Holy Spirit.

Now there are varieties of gifts, but the same Spirit; and there are varieties of service, but the same Lord; and there are varieties of working, but it is the same God who inspires them all in every one. To each is given the manifestation of the Spirit for the common good. To one is given through the Spirit the utterance of wisdom, and to another the utterance of knowledge according to the same Spirit, to another faith by the same Spirit, to another gifts of healing by the one Spirit, to another the working of miracles, to another prophecy, to another the ability to distinguish between spirits, to another various kinds of tongues, to another the interpretation of tongues. All these are inspired by one and the same Spirit, who apportions to each one individually as he wills.

Have you heard about the man who had some problems and decided to leave the ministry? He ran into trouble, however, when he couldn't find other work. Finally, in desperation, he took a job at the local zoo. The gorilla had died, and since it had been the children's favorite animal, the zoo officials decided to put someone in a gorilla costume until a real replacement could be found.

It was the minister's job to don the costume, hop around the cage, and entertain the kids. To his amazement, he found it the best job he'd ever held. He was getting more attention than he ever had in the pulpit. He could eat all he wanted. There was no stress—no complaints, no committees, no deadlines, no pressures. And he could take a nap in the sun any time—it was all part of the act.

One day as he hopped up and down, he felt so frisky he decided to try the trapeze. But as he swung high, he lost his grip, flew over the bars, and landed in the next cage! Stunned and dazed, he looked up and saw a ferocious lion charging right at him. Of course, in his panic, he forgot he was supposed to be a gorilla and screamed, "Help! Help!"

To which the lion said, "Hey, buddy, be quiet! I'm a minister too!"

Wouldn't it be something if every one of us could say that and mean it: "Hey! I'm a minister *too!*"

A bishop recently told of visiting a small church in the Midwest which had a banner hanging in the sanctuary with these words: *You are one of 203 ministers in this church.* What if each one of us said: "I'm a minister too" and served like a minister? What would it do to our church, to our city, to our world?

That's what happened at Pentecost. The Holy Spirit came and the disciples said, "Hey, we're ministers, too!" And they took up Christ's ministry and turned the world upside down.

This is what the Apostle Paul meant when he said that we are members one of another. Remember how he put it: "Now there are varieties of gifts, but the same Spirit;

and there are varieties of service, but the same Lord; and there are varieties of working, but it is the same God who inspires them all in every one" (I Cor. 12:5).

You may remember the movie *Angel in My Pocket,* about a minister and his family. There is a delightful scene in which the family has just moved to a new town and the preacher's small boy is getting acquainted with another boy.

The other boy asks: "What does your dad do for a living?"

The preacher's kid answers proudly, "He's a minister—*ordained!*"

The other boy, not to be outdone, proudly replies, "Well, my dad's in the hardware business—*ordained!*"

Now, that little boy unknowingly put his finger on the truth. The truth is that *all Christians*—whether in the hardware business or the ordained ministry—are called of God to minister in Christ's name. Some of us have had a bishop lay hands on our heads, but all of us have felt God's touch on our hearts. We are all called to be ministers!

What if we all responded to that call? What if we all took it seriously? What could happen? What *would* happen? If each one of us related to our church as if we were ministers, what impact would that have on our worship services, on our Sunday schools, on our budgets, on our outreach programs, on our caring ministries? You see, the point is this: That's precisely the way it ought to be.

When it's time to worship . . .

What would happen if we all said, "Hey! I'm a minister too!"

I remember a story about a mother who went upstairs to wake her son one Sunday morning.

She said to him, "Get up and get ready now. It's almost time to go to church. Rise and shine!"

He pulled the covers up over his shoulder and turned away. "I don't want to go today."

She said, "Come on, son, we always go to church."

He answered, "I'm tired. I want to sleep in. Sunday morning is the only time I get to sleep in."

"You can sleep some other time. We are going to church today," she told him.

With that, the son bolted upright. "Give me one good reason why we need to go to church today!"

"I'll give you *three* reasons," she replied. "First of all, it's for you. Second, it's a habit in our family. We always go to church! And third, *you* are the minister!"

I'm trying to plant an indelible thought in your mind that will flash on every Sunday morning when you are trying to decide whether to go to church. I hope this thought will flash again and again, like a brilliant neon sign, *every* Sunday morning: "Hey—I'm a minister too! I need to be there! I'm needed there; I'm part of it; I'm responsible for it! I help to make it happen! It's my ministry too!"

Some years ago, I was counseling with a young couple. They were having an argument every weekend over whether to go to church.

"That's interesting," I said to them, "because we never have that problem at our house. We made that decision a long time ago. We just decided to go every Sunday. It saves a lot of time and energy."

"That's different," they said. "You're the minister."

But is it different? I'm not so sure it is. I honestly

believe that I would come to church even if I weren't the minister. Millions of Christian people across the face of the earth have made that decision—they go to church every Sunday because they genuinely believe that they are ministers, too.

When it's time for Sunday school . . .

What would happen if we all said, "Hey! I'm a minister too!"

Have you heard about the little boy who came to Sunday school for the first time? He was a very imaginative young man and was greatly impressed by the story of Eve's creation out of Adam's rib. A couple of days later, he was running too hard and felt a pain in his side.

"Oh my goodness," he said to his mother, "I think I'm gonna have a wife!"

Sometimes we get it all mixed up, but if we hear it long enough and often enough, it falls into place.

I know a man who has an incredible commitment to our Sunday school program and to his class. He is totally dedicated to that class. One Sunday morning a few years ago, he put his car in reverse and backed out of his driveway—only to discover that his transmission was on the blink. It would not go into any gear but reverse!

What would you have done in that situation? Let me tell you what he did. *He backed all the way to Sunday school!* Now, you may question the safety factor there, but you can only admire that kind of commitment—an amazing dedication to Sunday school because he feels a sense of ministry.

Do you? What would our Sunday school be like, if every member were just like you?

When a problem needs solving . . .

What would happen if we all said, "Hey! I'm a minister too."

Some years ago Harry Emerson Fosdick preached a sermon titled "Are You Part of the Problem or Part of the Solution?" He indicated that as Christian people, our calling is to be part of the solution. We are to use our energies not to cause problems, but to solve them.

This means that if I'm walking across the front lawn of our church (as I did a few Sunday mornings ago) and see two beer cans and a half full whiskey bottle littering the yard, what do I do? I pick them up. I don't say, "That's not my job!" I don't murmur or complain. I clean it up because that helps God's kingdom.

Now, it can be a little awkward to walk into church on Sunday morning holding two beer cans and a whiskey bottle! Then there's another problem—whose trash can do you put them in?

We are all called to be God's ministers, and we are to give our energies to solving problems, not creating them. Going to church, studying in Sunday school, solving problems—it's a ministry we share.

When someone is hurting . . .

What would happen if we all said, "Hey! I'm a minister too!"

Some years ago, a friend of mine was working as a bank executive. As she walked past one of the offices, she glanced in and saw a young woman sitting at her desk, crying. She went in to see if she could help.

"Nothing's that bad," she said. "Tell me about it!"

The younger woman explained: "My mother died about a month ago. And I became engaged last night. I'm going to be married. I need to plan a wedding, and I don't know what to do. I don't have a mother to help me."

"Oh yes you do!" my friend said. "I'll be your mother!"

And as they hugged each other, an incredible friendship was born—all because one person saw somebody hurting and said, "Hey! I'm a minister too!"

12

When You Face
the Demands of Love

Mark 10:46-52 And they came to Jericho; and as he was leaving Jericho with his disciples and a great multitude, Bartimaeus, a blind beggar, the son of Timaeus, was sitting by the roadside. And when he heard that it was Jesus of Nazareth, he began to cry out and say, "Jesus, Son of David, have mercy on me!" And many rebuked him, telling him to be silent; but he cried out all the more, "Son of David, have mercy on me!" And Jesus stopped and said, "Call him." And they called the blind man, saying to him, "Take heart; rise, he is calling you." And throwing off his mantle he sprang up and came to Jesus. And Jesus said to him, "What do you want me to do for you?" And the blind man said to him, "Master, let me receive my sight." And Jesus said to him, "Go your way; your faith has made you well." And immediately he received his sight and followed him on the way.

In the Gospel of Mark the story of Jesus' dramatic encounter with blind Bartimaeus in Jericho takes up only seven verses of Scripture, and yet within those seven verses, we see the crux of the Christian gospel in a swiftly drawn portrait of Christian love. Here Jesus portrays the ways Christians are called to love other people.

Now, love is difficult to define, as we all know, but it can be *demonstrated,* and that is precisely what Jesus does here. He demonstrates Christian love—the kind of love needed in our homes, in our marriages, in our

106

friendships; in our relations with our co-workers, our neighbors, our acquaintances, even strangers.

In this powerful story, we see the anatomy of Christian love. Obviously, Bartimaeus has heard about Jesus. He senses that this is his moment, and when Jesus comes near he begins to cry out urgently: "Jesus, Son of David, have mercy on me!"

Suddenly Jesus stops. He turns around. Somehow, over the noise of the crowd, he has heard the poignant cry. And Jesus calls for him.

Bartimaeus throws his cloak aside; he springs up and makes his way through the crowd to Jesus.

Notice that Jesus is not presumptuous or arrogant or possessive. He never romps over people. He does not force himself on people. He does not pompously pronounce what Bartimaeus needs. No, he is very low key.

Humbly he asks, *"What do you want me to do for you?"*

And when Bartimaeus answers, *"I want to be able to see!"* Jesus says to him, *"Your faith has made you well."* The Scripture tells us that Bartimaeus then followed Jesus on the way.

What do we learn from this powerful story? There is so much here. Obviously, we could go in a number of different directions. We could look at the matter of healing, how Jesus healed Bartimaeus and how healing happens today. Or we could consider the special qualities of Bartimaeus that jump out of this story—his persistence, perseverance, boldness, determination, faith, his sensitivity to the uniqueness of the moment, his unwillingness to give in to the fear of embarrassment or his ability to seize an opportunity. Or we could point out that this great story sums up the good news of our faith:

- Our Need—We, like Bartimaeus, are blind.

- God's Action—God can heal us, restore our sight, give us a new vision.

- Our Response—Like Bartimaeus, we can follow him on the way.

But I want to zero in on what this story teaches us about love. Love is a many-splendored thing! We see this graphically in the touching encounter between Jesus and blind Bartimaeus. This story suggests several qualities of Christian love.

Christian love means
valuing other people personally.

"Love? What do you mean by love?" shouts the cynic. "The word has lost its meaning. We've used it too freely, too frequently, too lightly! We've tossed it about for every sort of feeling, from the mildest preference to the wildest passion. We 'love' potato chips and Mother Teresa. We 'love' pepperoni pizza and Robert Redford. We 'love' the Lakers and the Red Sox and the Oilers—when they are winning. We love our children, our churches—and antique furniture. We love our parents—and peanut butter. Do you see what I'm getting at?" cries the cynic. "Love, as a concept, has lost its identity. *Love,* as a word, has lost its definition."

Well, if you ever feel that way, fuzzy and confused about what love is, remember Jesus. He shows us what love is really all about! He reminds us that love means valuing other people. Think about that for a moment. *To love is to value!* If the word *love* seems overused or worn or misunderstood, then try putting the word *value* in its place. You know, that works pretty well: To love God with all your heart, soul, mind, and strength means to *value* God more than anything else in the world. To love your neighbor as yourself means to *value* your neighbor's life as much as you value your own.

Tonight when you tuck your children into bed, or today when you say "So long" to someone you love, or tomorrow in conversation with a prized co-worker, or next Valentine's Day, or whenever you want to express something special to someone you care for, try it! Say, "I value you so much!" And see what kind of response you get.

Jesus valued Bartimaeus personally! On his way to the cross, he stopped for Bartimaeus! That was his way of saying, "You count! You matter! You are worth something! You are valuable! You are important to me! You are a valued child of God, and I care about you personally!"

We see something very special here in Jesus, and something very special about Christian love: It is intensely *personal!* It is not enough to spout high-sounding words of love into the air. Real Christian love demands that we get personal.

Jesus shows us here that it is simply not enough to love humankind. Our task, our calling—indeed, our privilege, is to love *people,* to love specific *persons.* Or to put it another way, to value other people personally. That leads us to a second thought.

Christian love is all-inclusive.

Light a candle and it will give its light to everyone in the room. It is not selective. It shines for all. It includes all, and that's the way love is. Love reaches out to do good to all people, even the unlovable.

The crowd tried to silence Bartimaeus. "Be quiet!" they said. "Don't bother the Master! He doesn't have time for you!" But you see, they were so wrong. Here Jesus teaches us one of the most important aspects of Christian love. He stops to help Bartimaeus, a poor blind beggar no one else seems to care about. And in so doing, he underscores the beauty of all-inclusive love, the beauty of seeing everyone we meet as a child of God, a person of integrity and worth.

Recently I ran across a powerful ancient legend which I think expresses well what I am saying:

> A holy man's disciple asked, "How can I know when the dawn has broken; when the darkness has fled? It must be the moment when I can tell a sheep from a dog."
>
> But the holy man answered, "No!"
>
> The disciple then asked, "Is it then that moment when I can tell a peach from a pomegranate?"
>
> The holy man answered, "No, none of these. Until the moment when you can gaze in the face of a man or a woman and say, 'You are my brother, you are my sister.' Until then, there is no dawn; there is only darkness!"

First, Christian love means valuing other people personally. *Second,* it is all-inclusive, seeing and responding to every person we meet as a brother or sister for whom Christ came.

Christian love is not domineering.

Maybe this is why some of the books we see in our bookstores today bother me. I just can't get in my mind the picture of Jesus rushing to a bookstore to buy a book titled *Negotiating from Power* or *Winning by Intimidation.* Somehow these ideas seem diametrically opposed to the spirit of Christ.

Please notice that when Jesus comes face to face with Bartimaeus, he doesn't grab him by the collar and say, "I know what you need! I know what you want." No! Courteously, graciously, gently, humbly, Jesus asks, "What do you want me to do for you?" He lets Bartimaeus tell him what he wants.

I think many married couples make a tragic mistake at this point. During courtship, they are kind, patient, courteous, thoughtful, considerate. But they come back from the honeymoon drawing the battle lines, worrying about who is in control, trying to dominate each other. They forget that Christian love is never domineering. Jesus shows us that dramatically when he says to Bartimaeus, *"What do you want me to do for you?"*

Christian love is self-giving and sacrificial.

It means to give yourself to other people. It means to go out on a limb for others. Christian love is not just something you feel. It's something you do for the sake of others. Bartimaeus was crying for help. Jesus knew his need and came to the rescue.

Have you heard about a little twelve-year-old African boy who lived with his family in a small village? His name was Lawi. One day as Lawi was baby-sitting with his little brother while the other members of the family were at work in the sugarcane fields, their little hut caught fire and was quickly enveloped in flames.

Lawi was outside, but remembering his little brother,

he jumped up and ran into the blazing hut, only to find
the baby trapped by a burning rafter which had fallen
on him. Hurriedly, Lawi worked to free his brother. He
had trouble getting him loose as the flames danced
about his head. Finally, he freed him. He picked him
up, carried him outside, and revived him just as the hut
caved in.

By this time the villagers had gathered outside the
smoldering remains. They had been too frightened to
go inside or do anything to help, and they were
tremendously impressed with the courage of young
Lawi.

They congratulated him for his heroic efforts: "Lawi,
you are very brave. Weren't you frightened? What were
you thinking as you ran into the burning hut?"

Lawi answered, "I wasn't thinking of anything. I just
heard my little brother crying!"

How long has it been since you heard your brother or
sister crying? How long has it been since you stopped
and did something about it?

Now, don't miss the conclusion of that great story in
Mark 10. After Bartimaeus received his sight, he
followed Jesus on the way! See what this means?
Bartimaeus was so moved, so touched, so inspired, so
changed by the love Christ gave to him that he wanted
to be a part of that love. He wanted to pass it on! He
wanted to go out now and give that love to other people!

That is precisely your calling and mine—to love every
person we see just as Jesus loved Bartimaeus that day.
Facing up to the demands of love, and living in that
Spirit, can only make us better!

13

When You Have a Spiritual Checkup

Matthew 7:15-20 "Beware of false prophets, who come to you in sheep's clothing but inwardly are ravenous wolves. You will know them by their fruits. Are grapes gathered from thorns, or figs from thistles? So, every sound tree bears good fruit, but the bad tree bears evil fruit. A sound tree cannot bear evil fruit, nor can a bad tree bear good fruit. Every tree that does not bear good fruit is cut down and thrown into the fire. Thus you will know them by their fruits.

A friend sent me a fascinating article about how times have changed. The article, "Class of 1938 B.C. [before computers]," was written by Nardi Reeder Campion, who graduated from Wellesley College in 1938. Here is part of it:

With a 45th reunion comes a new phase of competition, the one described by Woody Allen when he said, "Ninety percent of life is just showing up."

But change is the name of the game. Consider. Graduates of the class of 1938 were . . . before television. Before penicillin, polio shots, antibiotics and Frisbees. Before frozen food, Nylon, Dacron, Xerox, Kinsey. We were before radar, flourescent lights, credit cards and ballpoint pens. For us, time-sharing meant togetherness, not computers; a chip meant a piece of wood; hardware meant hardware, and software wasn't even a word.

We were before . . . air travel went commercial; almost no one flew across the country, and translatlantic flights belonged to Lindbergh and Amelia Earhart. Before Israel and the United Nations. Before India, Pakistan, Indonesia, the Philippines, and Iceland were independent. Since our graduation, 92 countries—48 of them African—have become independent nations. . . .

We were before pantyhose and drip-dry clothes. Before ice makers and dishwashers, clothes driers, freezers and electric blankets. . . . Before Hawaii and Alaska became states. Before men wore long hair and earrings and women wore tuxedoes.

We were before Leonard Bernstein, yogurt, Ann Landers, plastics, hair dryers, the 40-hour week and the minimum wage. . . .

Closets were for clothes, not for coming out of . . . bunnies were small rabbits and rabbits were not Volkswagens. We were before Grandma Moses and Frank Sinatra. . . .

We were before Batman, *Grapes of Wrath,* Rudolph the Rednosed Reindeer, Stuart Little and Snoopy. Before DDT and vitamin pills . . . disposable diapers, Q. E. One, Jeeps, the Jefferson Memorial and the Jefferson nickel. . . .

When we were in college, pizzas, Cheerios, frozen orange juice, instant coffee, and McDonald's were unheard of. We thought *fast* food was what you ate during Lent.

We were before . . . Chiquita Banana. Before FM radio, tape recorders, electric typewriters, word processors, Muzak, electronic music, disco dancing—and that's not all bad.

In our day cigarette smoking was fashionable, grass was mowed, coke was something you drank, and pot was something you cooked in. We were before . . . coin vending machines, jet planes, helicopters, interstate highways. . . .

In our time there were 5-and-10-cent stores where you could buy things for 5 and 10 cents. For just one nickel you could ride the subway, or ride the ferry, or make a phone call, or buy a Coke, or buy two copies of *The Boston Globe* and get change, or buy enough stamps to mail one letter and two postcards. You could buy a new Chevy coupe for $659, but who could afford that in 1938? Nobody. A pity, too, because gas was 11 cents a gallon.

Sometimes it's quite natural and enjoyable to be nostalgic. Oh, how we like to reminisce about the good old days. But don't forget that someone once defined *nostalgia* as a matter of recalling the fun without reliving the pain!

An important ingredient in remembering the past is bringing it forward for a fresh evaluation of our lives. What have we been doing? How can we do better? Where in our personal lives do we need improvement? There is something very spiritual about that. Every now and then, we all need a spiritual "checkup."

Checkups are a part of life in our land. We go to doctors and dentists for periodic examinations. We take our cars to a mechanic for occasional tune-ups. Tests are given in school to be sure the students are really learning. So in our spiritual lives, we need a faith checkup every now and then.

Perhaps you have heard about the boy who went into a drugstore and called a lady named Mrs. Johnson.

He said, "Mrs. Johnson, do you need a good yard boy? I'm a hard worker."

Mrs. Johnson replied, "No thank you, I already have a fine young man who takes excellent care of my yard."

But the young boy persisted: "Does he get there on time? Does he charge a fair rate? Is he neat? Is he conscientious?"

Mrs. Johnson answered, "I do appreciate your interest, young man, but I am most pleased with the yard boy I now have. He is exceptionally good!"

The boy thanked her and hung up. The druggist had overheard the conversation and was impressed.

He said, "Wait a minute, son. I didn't know you were looking for a job. I'll hire you! I can give you a job right here in my drugstore!"

To which the boy replied, "Oh, no, thank you. I already have a great job! You see, I *am* Mrs. Johnson's yard boy. I was just checking up on myself!"

We all need to do that occasionally, don't we? We need to check up on ourselves to see how we are doing. That's what I would like for us to do now—have a checkup on our spiritual lives: "How am I doing as a Christian? Is my life-style worthy to earn the name Christian? Do I feel close to God? Does my faith work?"

Jesus said, "You will know them by their fruits." In the Sermon on the Mount, he said, "Every sound tree bears good fruit, but the bad tree bears evil fruit." Well—be honest now—how do you measure up? What kind of fruit is your life bearing these days?

Does your faith
give you confidence for living?

Does your faith really strengthen you? Does it give you a sense of assurance and victory? Does your faith help you stand up to life, stand up to the tensions, pressures, and stresses of this world? Does your faith make you hopeful, radiant, confident? You see, if we really believe what we sing in our hymns, discuss in our Sunday school classes, preach from our pulpits—if we really believe it—then we can be confident! We don't need to become so ruffled when things go awry.

Yet the truth is that many of us who ought to know better, who ought to have more faith, run scared all the time. We are chronic worriers—worried about the skeletons of the past, the demands of the present, and the mysteries of the future. We are worried, frustrated, and depressed by the threats, problems, and busyness of life. But the Christian faith says to us that we can be confident!

During the filming of the movie classic *Quo Vadis*, Deborah Kerr, one of the stars, was asked by a newspaper reporter, "During the scene when you were in the arena facing the lions, were you afraid?"

She answered, "Oh no! I wasn't afraid at all! You see, I had read the script, and I knew Robert Taylor would come and save me!"

As Christians, we don't need to be afraid, because we know God is with us! Emmanuel—"God with us"! He will not desert us. Nothing, not even death, can separate us from him. So we can be radiantly confident—not scared or anxiety-ridden, but confident! Ask yourself now: "Does my faith give me confidence for the living of these days?"

Does your faith make you more loving?

Love is the single most distinctive characteristic of the Christian faith, and probably the best test of your spiritual temperature. Jesus believed that. He called *love* the most reliable sign of Christian discipleship. How is it with you? Where do you stand? Are you more loving now than you were at this time last year?

Not long ago my psychologist friend Robert Minniear, being interviewed on television, said something that fascinated me: "If you really want to be happy, then pretend for one month that every person you meet is the most important person in the world—that is, relate to everybody you see as if he or she were the most important person in the world!!"

I thought, "That's a good idea." And then suddenly it hit me! I realized something—that the Christian faith calls us to an even higher plateau! It tells us to treat every person we meet as if he or she were Christ himself! Remember how Jesus put it: "Inasmuch as you did it to one of the least of these, you did it to me." Ask yourself: "Does my faith make me more loving?"

Does your faith keep on growing?

Listen now! Be honest! Have you grown in your faith recently? How many *new* spiritual insights did you experience in the last twelve months? How much of the Scriptures did you read? How much time did you spend in prayer? The word *disciple* means "learner." Are you still learning? In counseling with young couples who are about to be married, I say to them: "Go into marriage as *learners!*" Try every day to learn more and more about marriage, more and more about love, more and more about life, more and more about communication, more and more about each other, more and more about God. The same thing could be said to every Christian. Go into it as learners; never stop growing. Ask yourself: "Does my faith keep on growing?"

Does your faith work in practical daily living?

To be good at all, our faith must work in the work-a-day world. Voltaire once said that some of his contemporaries were "like an oven: always heating, but never cooking anything!" Real faith does more than warm our hearts. It cooks! It works now!

Remember the man who had been a hopeless drug addict until he met Christ? He became a Christian and was changed dramatically. And he had a vivid memory of what his life had been like before the Christian faith literally had saved him.

In a discussion one day, he heard a co-worker say something like this: "Religion is a delusion. It doesn't work."

The former addict responded, "Then thank God for the delusion! It has put shoes on my children's feet, bread on my table, and peace and joy in hearts where before there was only hell! The Christian faith does work! It's working for me! It's saving my life!"

Ask yourself: "Does my faith work in practical daily living?"

Does your faith give you a sense of partnership with God?

Go into life today and every day, saying over and over within yourself, "I am a child of God. God is with me. I am God's partner! I am working *with* God and *for* God, and He is working through me." If you take up that spirit of partnership with God, your life will be changed incredibly. It will change the way you work, the way you speak, your tone of voice, the way you relate to others, your energy level, your outlook, your attitudes—and life will be better for you because that's the way God meant it to be. Dag Hammarskjold said it wonderfully in his daily prayer:

Give me a pure heart—that I may see Thee,
A humble heart—that I may hear Thee,
A heart of love—that I may serve Thee,
A heart of faith—that I may abide in Thee.

Well, how did you do? How do you measure up? Does your faith make you more confident? Does your faith make you more loving? Does your faith keep on growing? Does your faith work in the practical world? Does your faith give you a sense of partnership with God? If you can answer yes to all these questions, you are in pretty good shape spiritually. If not, then you need to spend some time with the Great Physician! A spiritual checkup can tell you whether you're getting bitter or better.

14

When Life Is Stressful

Matthew 25:31-40 "When the Son of man comes in his glory, and all the angels with him, then he will sit on his glorious throne. Before him will be gathered all the nations, and he will separate them one from another as a shepherd separates the sheep from the goats, and he will place the sheep at his right hand, but the goats at the left. Then the King will say to those at his right hand, 'Come, O blessed of my Father, inherit the kingdom prepared for you from the foundation of the world; for I was hungry and you gave me food, I was thirsty and you gave me drink, I was a stranger and you welcomed me, I was naked and you clothed me, I was sick, and you visited me, I was in prison and you came to me.' Then the righteous will answer him, 'Lord, when did we see thee hungry and feed thee, or thirsty and give thee drink? And when did we see thee a stranger and welcome thee, or naked and clothe thee? And when did we see thee sick or in prison and visit thee?' And the King will answer them, 'Truly, I say to you, as you did it to one of the least of these my brethren, you did it to me.' "

There is a story about a man who walked backward across the United States. He started in California and ended in New York.

At the end of his journey, someone asked, "What was the hardest part of your trip? What was the single most difficult thing? Was it the desert, or the mountains, or the rivers?"

"No," the man answered. "It was the sand in my shoes!"

This story has an obvious meaning for most of us in this hectic, overdriven world in which we live. Today we are threatened far more seriously, in both health and character, by a multitude of little strains than by the occasional and spectacular big ones. In fact, most of us manage the major emergencies of life quite well. The great trials—sorrow, tragedy, hardship and bereavement—we handle with poise and strength, only to be worn down by the little things. When a crisis comes, how admirably we rise to the occasion! We are more likely to be taken down and torn apart by the "sand in our shoes."

A few years ago a young man came to see me. Talk about major emergencies and crises! This young man had had his share and then some. Over the last few years his parents had been killed in a car wreck, his daughter had suffered a prolonged illness, his wife had had emotional problems, his house had burned down, and his mother-in-law had been taken into their home with terminal cancer. He had cared for her tenderly until her death.

Through all these tremendous problems, he had been a tower of strength, an inspiration to everyone in the community. But the morning he came to my office, he was a wreck. He was depleted, depressed, devastated. Why? That morning his boss had pointed out that his sales were a little behind last year's. It crushed him! He had withstood all those big tragedies, but that small critique, that brief comment, that little thing had ripped him apart! That's often the way it happens.

Think about it. What destroys marriages? Little

things! What alienates families? Little things! What is the difference between success and failure, victory and defeat? Little things! What cripples a church more than any other factor? Little things! If you see a person, a marriage, a family, a business, a church, a community, a nation, limping along, you can count on it—the problem is sand in the shoes!

Jesus recognized the importance of little things, and he told a story to make the point. He put his parable in the setting of the Great Judgment. Some of the people were on the right and some were on the left. Some received a great blessing; the others missed out. Why? The distance between them was really not so great, but their destinies were poles apart.

Jesus explained that the difference in destinies was caused by little things—a sandwich to a hungry man, clothes to a needy person, a cup of water to one who is thirsty, a kindness to a stranger, a visit to someone sick or in prison. That was all—just little things. Yet these little things, and the way we handle them or mishandle them, makes all the difference.

Little Worries

Little worries, nagging anxieties, frustrating annoyances, can destroy us. We seem to handle the big concerns pretty well, but the little worries are the sand in our shoes. There is a lot of wisdom in this prayer: "Lord, we can handle the elephants, but please deliver us from these gnats."

Harry Emerson Fosdick told this interesting story. On the slope of Long's Peak in Colorado lies the ruin of a gigantic tree. Naturalists tell us it had stood for some four hundred years. It was a seedling when Columbus arrived at San Salvador; it was half-grown when the Pilgrims settled at Plymouth. During the course of its long life, it had been struck by lightning fourteen times and innumerable avalanches and storms had hit it, lashed it, and thundered past it. But it survived them all.

In the end, however, it fell. Why? Because an army of tiny beetles ate their way through the bark and gradually destroyed the tree with their incessant attacks. A forest giant that age could not wither, lightning could not blast, storms could not subdue, fell at last before beetles so small you could crush them with your finger.

Little worries are like those tiny beetles—small, but always there, attacking incessantly, continually burrowing their way into the heart and devastating our inner strength until we collapse.

Little Pressures

Little ever-present tensions pull at us till sometimes our nerves are stretched beyond the breaking point.

Did you hear about the woman who had a nervous breakdown in church when the choir sang "Awake My Soul, Stretch Every Nerve"? She said everything else in her life had been saying that to her, and she just couldn't take it when the choir kept repeating it too! Stretch every nerve—we know about that, don't we? But have you thought about it like this—there is a new kind of "nerve stretching," a new kind of pressure.

Remember the spectacular hardships of our ancestors. Look what they were up against. Their troubles were big ones; they were fighting to survive! They were doing battle against big things—cold, famine, pestilence, wild animals, hostile neighbors. They had no supermarkets, no microwave ovens, no miracle drugs, no hospitals. Just putting food on the table was a major accomplishment.

We don't have those kind of pressures, but we do confront a newly arrived army of beetles. We have a different kind of sand in our shoes. Some years ago, a doctor in New York said that civilization's three major killers are not heart disease, cancer, and accidents, but calendars, telephones, and clocks—the tyranny of an accelerated life. There is an office building in Detroit nicknamed Ulcer Alley. We are being attacked by little pressures.

Once I read about a man who was tied down and the ants attacked him and devoured him. We feel tied down too. And little things are eating away at us: The friends who call us on the phone and talk and talk; the agents who are determined to sell us a new mop, even though we don't need one; the children who quarrel and will not do their lessons; the letters that must be answered before night, somehow; the iceman's short weight; the butcher's carelessness. All these little things are devouring us alive. Our eyes cannot see, our ears cannot hear, even our brains are being destroyed. Only the husks of us smile wearily on and on.

I once conducted a funeral for a young man who had committed suicide. I was intrigued by his story. He had completed his education and had done quite well. He had survived the death of his grandparents and the divorce of his parents. He had been in Vietnam and had survived the awful anguish of war. He came home, found a good job, and was so capable that he soon became the company's number-one troubleshooter, on call twenty-four hours a day.

But the constant pressures of work piled up—the responsibilities, the continual problems, the lack of sleep, the ringing telephone. Then he had a car wreck. No one was hurt, but he worried about being sued and about whether his insurance would be cancelled. The pressures mounted, the sand in his shoes grated, his nerves stretched, and one evening he shot himself. The daily pressures were just too much for him. Little worries, little pressures can wear us down and destroy us.

Little Resentments

Resentment, envy, jealousy—these may seem like little things, but the truth is that they are spiritual poisons. I like to think about the "three miles of love." In the first mile, we love the lovable, those who love us back. In the second mile, we love the unlovable, those who don't love us back. In the third mile (the most difficult), we love those who outdo us, those who succeed where we fail, those who are more fortunate than we, those who win the election we wanted to win, those who get the girl we wanted, those who land the job we wanted—that is the love of the saints! Resentment, envy, and jealousy are so dangerous because they can slip up on the best of people.

Remember Oscar Wilde's famous story about the devil who comes upon a group of people tormenting a holy man. They are trying to break his spirit, but to no avail. He resists every temptation with poise and serenity. They tempt him with wine, food, beautiful women, money, and worldly pleasures, but the holy man is steadfast, unbending in his commitment.

Finally, after watching for a while, the devil says to the tempters, "Your methods are too crude, too obvious; permit me."

Then the devil walks over and whispers to the holy man, "Have you heard the news? Your brother has just been made bishop of Alexandria!" Immediately, a malignant scowl of jealousy clouds the formerly serene face of the holy man!

Jealousy—is that the sand in your shoes? Little worries, little pressures, little resentments can gnaw away at us incessantly and devastate us within. What can we do? How do we cope? How do we withstand the onslaught? Is there life after stress? Let me make some suggestions:

TRAVEL LIGHT. That is, decide what is really important to you and give your energies to those things. We can't do everything, so we must decide what really matters and weed out all the rest.

TAKE ONE STEP AT A TIME. Do one thing at a time. Live one day at a time. Remember the old story about the clock. It figured out that it would have to tick more than 31 million times in one year. Overwhelmed by that thought, the clock just quit. Until someone reminded it that it didn't need to tick them all at once—just one tick at a time.

Jesus spoke about this in the Sermon on the Mount. He said, "Don't be so anxious about tomorrow." Just take it one day at a time, one thing at a time, one step at a time.

RELAX YOUR SOUL IN GOD. Jesus' parable of the sower speaks to this. The idea is to sow the seed the best you can and trust God to bring the harvest. It doesn't matter if the odds are against you. It doesn't matter that things sometimes seem hopeless. It doesn't matter how bleak the outlook. Don't worry about it. Just sow the seed and leave the rest to God.

That's what it means to relax our souls in God. We just sow the seed. We do the best we can, then trust God to bring everything out right. When life gets stressful, we can get better by leaning on him.

15

When You Are Confused in the Religious Marketplace

Matthew 17:1-5, 14-16, 18-21

And after six days Jesus took with him Peter and James and John his brother, and led them up a high mountain apart. And he was transfigured before them, and his face shone like the sun, and his garments became white as light. And behold, there appeared to them Moses and Elijah, talking with him. And Peter said to Jesus, "Lord, it is well that we are here; if you wish, I will make three booths here, one for you and one for Moses and one for Elijah." He was still speaking, when lo, a bright cloud overshadowed them, and a voice from the cloud said, "This is my beloved Son, with whom I am well pleased; listen to him." . . .

And when they came [down] to the crowd, a man came up to him and . . . said, "Lord, have mercy on my son, for he is an epileptic and he suffers terribly; for often he falls into the fire, and often into the water. And I brought him to your disciples, and they could not heal him." And Jesus answered . . . "Bring him here to me." And Jesus rebuked him, and the demon came out of him, and the boy was cured instantly. Then the disciples came to Jesus privately and said, "Why could we not cast it out?" He said to them, "Because of your little faith. For truly, I say to you, if you have faith as a grain of mustard seed, you will say to this mountain, 'Move from here to there,' and it will move; and nothing will be impossible to you."

I n 1931, a baby boy was born in Indiana—a baby boy destined to become one of the most notorious religious leaders of our time. His name was Jim Jones! Jim Jones became an American cult leader who promised his followers a utopia in the jungles of South America. He proclaimed himself "messiah" of the People's Temple, a San Francisco-based evangelical group, and ultimately led his followers into a mass suicide known as the Jonestown Massacre, the Guyana Tragedy. It happened on November 18, 1978.

Earlier, Jones had gained a reputation as a charismatic churchman in Indiana. After moving to California, he apparently became obsessed with the exercise of power. In the face of mounting accusations by journalists and defectors from the cult that he was illegally diverting the income from cult members to his own use, Jones and hundreds of his followers emigrated to Guyana in 1974 and set up an agricultural commune called Jonestown. As ruler of the sect, Jones confiscated passports and millions of dollars, manipulating his followers with threats of blackmail, beatings, and death. He also staged bizarre rehearsals for a ritual mass suicide.

On November 17, 1978, U. S. Representative Leo Ryan of California arrived in Jonestown with a group of newsmen to conduct an unofficial investigation of alleged abuses. The next day, as Congressman Ryan's party and sixteen defectors from the cult prepared to leave from an airstrip near Jonestown, the group was attacked by armed men. When Jones learned that Ryan and four others had been killed and the others had escaped, he knew the jig was up and the authorities would be brought in, so he activated his mass-suicide plan. On November 18, 1978, Jim Jones commanded his followers to drink cyanide-laced punch. Strangely and inexplicably, the vast majority obeyed his command. Jones himself died of a gunshot wound, which may or may not have been self-inflicted. We don't know about that, but we do know that when Guyanese troops reached Jonestown the next day, they found 779 members of the Jim Jones cult dead! And almost 200 of them were children!

I thought of the Jonestown Massacre a few weeks ago when a twelfth-grade student asked me, "Is religion always good?"

Immediately, my mind flashed back to the Guyana Tragedy, and I said, "No! Religion is *not* always good. Some of the worst things that ever happened in human history were done because of religion. Some people think it doesn't matter what you believe as long as you believe something, but it does matter! It matters more than I can tell you. History has shown dramatically that wrongly motivated, mixed-up religion can be very destructive!"

Good religion is creative and constructive, and it enables people to do wonderful, God-like things. But bad religion is disastrous. It produces fanatics who are closed and negative, narrow-minded and sometimes cruel.

Does that bother you? Let me document it. Remember the Crusades, the Inquisition, the Salem witch hunts, the crucifixion of Jesus, to name just a few. Bloody wars, cruel persecutions, brutal rituals, human sacrifices, strange superstitions—all have taken place under the cloak of religion. And in our own time, we have seen acts of terrorism, bombings, skyjackings, mass suicides, kidnappings, blood baths, murders, violence, hostility, prejudice. Bizarre cults engage in brain-washing and mind manipulation to entice young people to reject their families, friends, and their career plans.

The point is clear: Religion can be very, very good. But misdirected, it can be very, very bad. Religion can produce a Moses, a Jesus, a Paul, a St. Francis, a Mother Teresa, or a John Wesley. But it also can produce a Jim Jones or a Charles Manson. When religious ideas are true, they save, heal, make whole. When they are false, they crush, destroy, devastate.

Some years ago when I was in high school, I had a good friend named Willie. Willie was one of those delightful characters who was always the life of the party. For those of you over thirty, he had what we used to call an Ipana smile. For those under thirty, he had a mouthful of Ultra-Brite teeth. And he was always grinning. Everybody liked Willie. He was a friend to everybody. He was the fellow (you know the type) who was forever broke, always borrowing a quarter in the school cafeteria, but somehow nobody seemed to mind. That was just "good old Willie." He could walk into a room and make people laugh and feel good. He had that special kind of happy charisma that is so unique.

But one day Willie "got religion"; unfortunately, it was the wrong kind. He changed completely, and, sadly, it was a change that was negative and debilitating. Within a few weeks, Willie had become so sanctimonious that everybody felt uncomfortable with him. Some even avoided him. He didn't smile anymore. He rarely spoke, and when he did, it was in a very pious tone. He carried a Bible under his arm and constantly preached a negative religion, laying it on in a holier-than-thou tone.

One day as we were sitting in the lunchroom, Willie came striding through very pompously, as though he were the perfect blend of John the Baptist, Simon Peter, Martin Luther, and Billy Graham, all rolled into one. Someone was heard to say, "You know, I liked him better before he got religion!"

Now obviously, I am for religion. I have committed my life to it. But I am also aware of an important point in the Scriptures—namely, as far as we know, Jesus never met an atheist. That is, his problems and conflicts were not with irreligious people; he was opposed and betrayed by *religious* people. Religious people can be God-like, but when their motives get mixed up, when their thoughts become confused or self-serving, they may nail somebody to a cross. Good religion will open you up like a flower; it will make you bloom with new life; it will set you free. But bad religion will cause you to wither and die; it can make you narrow and unbending, negative, self-righteous, closed-minded. Jesus said it like this: "If then the light in you is darkness, how great is the darkness!" (Matt. 6:23).

It's a tremendously important question then, isn't it? How do we tell the difference between good religion and bad religion? Let me list what I think are some basic qualities of good religion. I'm sure you can think of others. I just want to plant some seeds in your thinking so these thoughts can continue in your mind long after this moment.

But before getting into those qualities, let me remind you of life in the ancient marketplace. The ancient marketplace had an interesting motto: "Let the Buyer Beware!" In other words, "Watch out! Be cautious! Don't be gullible! You may be sold something for an outrageous price that you don't really want!" So let the buyer beware!

It seems to me that is a pretty good motto for the religious marketplace of our time. There are a lot of confusing religious ideas and appeals in our world today, all vying for our attention, all trying to win us to their way of thinking. So it's a good idea to be cautious in the religious marketplace. *Don't be gullible!* It's also my opinion that it's a good idea to stay close to the mainline churches—churches that are history-tested, time-honored, and trustworthy. Beware of the fly-by-night religious personality who zips into town with an easy one-step program to salvation and a few exotic gimmicks, and then just as quickly zips away, never to be seen again. Beware of those who try to steal you away from your church with smooth talk and pious smiles and cloaked innuendoes which suggest, ever so slyly, that the church you are now in just isn't quite as spiritual as they are. Let the buyer beware!

Now to the basic qualities of good religion.

Good religion keeps growing.

It is open to *new truths* from God.

Jim Jones closed the book on truth. He thought he was the only truth, and anyone who questioned him was punished cruelly. But you can see how wrong that is! A call to discipleship is a call to grow in the faith, to think, to stretch, to wonder, to probe, to love God with our minds. For this reason, we need to beware of any religion that shuts down thinking. We need to beware of any religion that says, "Here's what to believe. Learn this, accept this, swallow this. Don't ask questions, and don't bring up any new ideas!"

We also need to beware of being content with one dramatic religious experience. That was Simon Peter's temptation on the Mount of Transfiguration. There he experienced Jesus, Moses, and Elijah. It was wonderful, powerful, mind-boggling. He knew God was in that place, and he wanted to stay there on the mountaintop.

But Jesus probably said to him, "Peter, this has been good, but we can't stay here. We must move on! We must be open to new experiences with God at other times and in other places." Good religion keeps on growing. It's ever open to new truth from God. Religion is like a parachute; it works best when open! Bad religion, on the other hand, is closed, narrow, negative, stale, and afraid. Good religion says, "All truth is from God, so let me learn!" Bad religion says, "Don't confuse me with the facts. And if you don't do it my way, you are lost!" Good religion keeps on growing and learning. It is open, it does not close the book on truth.

Good religion works in daily life.

Good religion works *now*. It gives us confidence for living *now*! It makes us better people *now*! Good religion is not just an insurance policy for another day. Jesus came off the Mount of Transfiguration, walked right down into the valley, and healed an epileptic boy. So good religion is not just something that dwells on the past or longs for the future; it works *now,* speaks to us *now,* makes us whole *now!*

Bishop Arthur Moore loved to tell the story of a man who had been away from his home church for some years, involved in all kinds of shady practices and criminal activities. But when he came back to his home church and testimony-time came, he was ready.

He stood and said, "I'm so glad to be back in my own church, and I want to tell you that while it's true that I have beaten my wife, that I have deserted my children, that I have stolen and lied and done all manner of evil and served several terms in jail—but I want you to know, brothers and sisters, that not once, in all that time, did I ever lose my religion!"

Now, if your religion is nothing more than an insurance policy for heaven, if it has no effect on how you live and how you treat others *now,* then first of all, you are missing out on life. And second, you'd better check your motivation. Christianity is good religion because it works in day-to-day life.

Some years ago, Harry Emerson Fosdick received a letter from a young mother in which she told what happened when she moved into a new subdivision:

> We tried everything we could think of to make this place something other than a real-estate development. We tried organized recreation, community picnics, and square dancing. We formed a women's club and held bridge parties, and started a garden club. We had a parents' organization and evening discussion groups. We tried everything. But it was not until the church came that we

changed from a subdivision into a community and became real neighbors to one another.

(*Dear Mr. Brown,* 1961 , p. 150)

Good religion works now—in practical daily living. It gives us a sense of personal partnership with God. Good religion keeps on growing, and it works *now*.

Good religion makes us more loving.

This was Jesus' test. For him, *love* was the measuring-stick for good religion. For him, *love* was the most genuine, the most reliable, the most authentic sign of discipleship. Remember how Jesus put it in John 13:34-35: "A new commandment I give to you, that you love one another; even as I have loved you. . . . By this all men will know that you are my disciples."

And how dramatically the Apostle Paul might have put it: "What does it matter if you can speak in tongues? If you don't have love, it's not worth anything! And what does it matter if you can do miraculous things? Without love, it's all empty and worthless! And what does it matter if you can quote reams of Scripture and spout high-sounding theology into the air! Without love, it's only so much noise! Faith, hope, love abide, these three; but the greatest of these is *love*" (I Cor. 13:8-13, paraphrase). So put love first and make love your aim. That's what God wants you to do.

Now, if you have a religious experience and it makes you more loving, then, in my opinion, it is a valid experience; it's good religion. But if you have a religious experience that makes you narrow or hateful or judgmental or holier than thou, then, in my opinion, that is bad news, and bad religion! Bad religion is selfish. Good religion is self-giving. Bad religion says, "What's in it for me?" Good religion says, "What can I do for God and for others?" If you want to test your faith, just raise one question: "Does my faith make me more loving?" Good religion keeps growing. It works *now,* and it makes us more loving.

Good religion combines worship and service.

It combines the devotional life with social action. We see this dramatically in Scripture, because in the Transfiguration story we see outlined three different approaches to religion. First, there are the Pietists (symbolized here by Simon Peter) who say, "Let's stay here on the mountaintop. Let's just worship here and not get smudged by the problems of the world."

Second, there are the social activists (symbolized here by the disciples), who are down in the valley trying to heal, but they can't do it because they have no power; they have no power because they haven't been up on the mountain.

Third, there is the approach of Jesus. He combines the two. He puts worship and service together. He puts devotion and social action together. He goes up on the mountain to worship, then comes down into the valley to heal! Now, *that's good religion!*

If you feel confused or perplexed by the varied kinds of religions clammering for your attention and allegiance; if you feel bewildered about the difference between good religion and bad religion, bring your thoughts back home to Christianity's one unique fact—*Jesus of Nazareth.* He is our pattern, our blueprint, our measuring stick. For us as Christians, he is the real

test of good religion. In the poem "Our Master,"
Whittier put it like this:

> O Lord and Master of us all!
> Whate'er our name or sign,
> We own Thy sway, we hear Thy call,
> We test our lives by Thine. . . .
>
> We faintly hear, we dimly see,
> In differing phrase we pray;
> But, dim or clear, we own in Thee
> The Light, the Truth, the Way.